SIMON AND SCHUSTER • NEW YORK

Flight

to

Freedom

Illustrations by Juan Barberis

KENT DURDEN

SBN 671-21716-X
Library of Congress Catalog Card Number: 73-18113
Designed by Edith Fowler
Manufactured in the United States of America
1   2   3   4   5   6   7   8   9   10

To my wife, Judi

Author's Preface

In writing this narrative, I feel it necessary to illuminate the reader as to the background of the story. My previous book, *Gifts of an Eagle,* tells the story of Lady, a golden eagle who for sixteen years remained in captivity, in a close relationship with my father, Ed Durden. This second book also centers on Lady, this time following her as she seeks a new way of life in the wild.

Although many of the incidents related herein did happen and were witnessed, there is an element of the story that is fictionalized. In an effort to maintain authenticity throughout, I have used as sources of information the following: actual eyewitness accounts of Lady; known habits and traits as we observed her in captivity; known habits and traits of eagles in general as observed by other naturalists; actual events which may have directly or indirectly affected her; natural history of the area in which she now lives; and a careful speculation of incidents that could have occurred as she made the difficult transition to the wild.

I have striven to present the material in as factual and believable a way as possible in an effort to portray the life of this golden eagle in a nonfiction manner.

KENT DURDEN

There are three things too wonderful
for me to understand. One is the way
of an eagle through the sky . . .

—SOLOMON

chapter i

High above the oak-studded Santa Ynez Valley, two golden eagles soared on invisible rising currents of warm air. As they reached appropriate altitude, they set their wings and glided in a northerly direction. Once over a ridge they again soared upward on the uplifting air. It was obvious they were traveling and not hunting. The larger female allowed the male to lead, never leaving the circling pattern until he did, and then maintaining a position close behind him as they worked their way across the valley.

For the female, this was a momentous occasion. Her name was Lady, the name given her by her human companion, Ed Durden, over sixteen years before when she was brought to his home as a nestling. Lady had, in just the last hour, chosen to sever forever the warm relationship that existed between her and a human being. Now she was being drawn by an invisible force to follow this male eagle, a force beyond her understanding. Although she enjoyed her captive years and had been bonded to her human companion, the decision to leave had been the natural one.

If there was any feeling of confusion at leaving her human friend, it had been completely obliterated by the presence of her newfound mate.

Once again the two birds reached an altitude which allowed them to clear the next mountain ridge. Then the male left the pattern and resumed his northerly course. Lady immediately fell in behind him.

Although she was the larger of the two, which is the way in birds of prey, it was the male that had initiated this courtship. Actually, they had met a year before under quite different circumstances. On one of her regular flights from her home on the point, Lady had drifted across the valley several miles and unknowingly entered the territory of a pair of wild eagles. It was the male of the pair that saw her first. From his vantage point a thousand feet above, he plummeted down in a surprise attack. Only a quick maneuver on her part at the last instant saved her life. As the male swooped past he screamed an angry challenge and climbed to regain his advantage of altitude. The female of the pair arrived and took up the attack. But Lady had no intention of fighting, and with swift wingbeats she fled the area. The wild pair, seeing the intruder on the run, pulled up from another attack and circled. The fact that she fled was not a sign of cowardice, only a sign of recognition of territorial ownership. Once she had passed the invisible boundary, the wild eagles turned away and left her free to fly unmolested. Now, it was that very same male she followed so closely into the very territory from which she had been driven a year before. What strange circumstances had changed this relationship?

The male had been raised in a remote valley several hundred miles to the north in the foothills of the Sierra Nevada mountain range. For the first two years of his life he had remained within fifty miles of his home. But as he grew toward maturity he began to wander, usually in a southerly direction. By his fifth year, he had settled in the remote Sisquoc back country of Santa Barbara County in Southern California. There he met a passing female and together they established their territory. Over the years their territory remained stable until one spring a violent storm sent their nest and chick crashing down the steep cliff. After that experience they changed territories in order to find a more suitable nest site. Their new home area encompassed a hundred square miles of isolated Santa Ynez back country.

Although this territory extended westward into civilized areas, it afforded many secluded nesting sites in its northern portion. Most of the eagles' hunting activity was carried on in remote areas so they had little contact with man. There were times, however, when the female drifted westerly into the farm lands to hunt. The male, having had several frightening experiences with man, was nervous at his mate's boldness and usually remained at a safe height. He preferred to hunt in more secluded areas.

On her own, one of the female's bold hunting trips was to prove fatal. The male saw from high above that she was making an attack on a ground squirrel in a dry arroyo. Her path would take her over an embankment at low altitude. Hidden from her view were two hunters walking close to the bluff. The male tensed as he saw his mate approach the men. As her black form swept over the hunters, they whirled and raised their guns. The female saw, but too late. As she banked sharply, two shots rang out and one slug tore through her body, sending her crashing in a crumpled mass. Helpless and distraught, the male watched from above as the hunters stretched out the wings of his mate and examined their prize. With the fear of man reinforced in his mind, he turned away and mounted up to return to the safety of the back country.

For several days he glanced skyward for the familiar form of his mate. Golden eagles usually mate for life and only when one of a pair dies will the other seek a new partner. For nearly ten years he and his mate had been together. It was spring and already he had selected a nest site which she had accepted. Had she lived, she would have laid eggs within a few days. But it is not the way of the wild to ponder over losses. Now the desire to get a new mate was strong in him. He must find one.

For many years he had been aware of the large female that lived twenty miles across the valley. He could never understand her, however. He recognized her territory for he often saw her flight patterns, and once he had driven her from his own territory. The puzzling thing was that he never saw her mate. Adding to his confusion was the fact that her eyrie seemed to be with humans. Indeed, he had even seen her stand unafraid as a human touched her. For the male, these things were incomprehensible. But the fact remained that the female was there, and she apparently had no mate.

It was with great apprehension that he first approached Lady's hilltop. All morning he had been watching from an oak tree five miles away. Around midday he saw a man approach the cage in which the female lived. A door was opened and Lady flew out over the valley. As she mounted up the male watched. Then he too took to the air and, gaining altitude, he began to drift toward her. He had entered her territory and had to be cautious. Had she exercised her right to attack, he would have fled. But although she saw him, she gave no indication that she knew he was there. For the male this was encouragement. He drifted closer and passed within a hundred feet of her. For several minutes they circled. She was as cautious as he was. Though to human eyes it would have appeared that each bird was indifferent to the other, small signs, infinitely vague, passed between the two eagles.

The very fact that she allowed him near her was encouraging. On several occasions before, wild males had joined Lady's flight only to be driven away or ignored. This time it was different. The male uttered a series of short chirps as he passed near and Lady answered. He drifted north toward his own territory and she followed for nearly three miles. But then she pitched back toward her home with man, drawn by an invisible bond to the things that were familiar. The male headed back into his own territory, but instead of going deep into the back country, he again landed in the oak.

For the next week the wild eagle joined Lady every time she took to the air. The courtship progressed from the first tentative encounter to unabashedly open displays. These usually took place high in the air, miles from Lady's cage. Spectacular flight displays were performed by each bird. Loud calls accompanied the wild plunges through open space by each participant. Fantastic pull-outs produced loud claps as tormented feathers strained against the wind. Both birds were stimulated by each other's courtship displays. Nothing in nature is quite as wild and free and independent as the nuptial flights of eagles.

Each day the eagerness and anticipation for these encounters grew for both eagles. Still the male's shyness of man prevented him from coming too close to Lady's home. Once, after a series of nuptial displays, his excitement was so great that he momentarily forgot his fear and followed Lady nearly to her cage before turning away in alarm. Her excitement at this point was almost uncontrollable, and had not her human companion appeared, she would have left then.

Ten days after the first encounter, just before dawn, the male roused and began to preen his feathers. From his oak perch he could barely see Lady's cage across the misty valley. The adobe house beyond looked quiet. Silently he launched off the tree and dropped down the slope to gain speed. The air was still and he had a difficult time gaining the necessary altitude to cross the valley.

His attraction to Lady was by now so strong that his fear of man was temporarily overcome. Gradually he came closer and passed over her cage calling loudly. From inside the cage he heard her response. Quickly and gracefully, he whipped around an oak and landed on a stump in front of the cage. Lady was perched inside, just a scant ten feet away. Although her calls were excited and expressed the desire to mate, she could not get out. For twenty minutes their loud calls shattered the silence of early morning. Then a slight movement in the house a hundred yards away sent the male plummeting off the hill to land, minutes later, on a power pole a quarter mile away. For two hours he watched Lady; then he disappeared over the valley.

It was nearly midday when Lady flew from the point for the last time and mounted up to follow the wild male. Instinct had told her it was time to leave.

Now the two eagles were high over the valley. For the moment, their flight consisted only of a deliberate pattern of soaring for altitude and gliding for distance. Gradually the point across the valley where Lady's cage stood became more distant. Several times as she swung about, her eyes perceived the familiar figure of the man standing alone on the point watching. But she glanced back for no other reason than for reference—the point being only one of several landmarks with which she kept herself oriented as she flew.

Although she was entering alien territory—a territory she had often pierced with her powerful eyes but had never been allowed to enter—the presence of her mate calmed any anxiety she might have had. In some mysterious way she knew it was permissible.

The fact that Lady had spent her entire life in close association with man would have handicapped her immensely had she left home to explore alone. Since she had no fear of man she would, no doubt, have been shot by someone as she perched near habitation. But with this wild mate, whom we shall call *Patu* because it is an American Indian word for protector, she would never approach man again. Even now as they crossed a ridge a ranch pickup appeared. Lady would have passed within a hundred feet had she been alone, but Patu turned away in alarm and led her around the ridge at a safe distance.

Below them a single ranch road wound its way up the valley. Scattered heads of cattle indicated that this was a working ranch. The country was hilly, with oak-covered slopes rising five hundred feet above the valley floor. The lengthening shadows of late afternoon cast strange patterns across the green earth. Along the westerly side and the north end of the large valley, rocky ridges and cliffs provided ex-

19

cellent nesting and perching sites. The valley floor was pock-marked with the holes of ground squirrels. The trails of rabbits could be seen crisscrossing the sage slopes. This was indeed eagle country and Lady's excitement grew as she scanned the ground below.

Suddenly Patu half closed his wings and dropped in a steep glide toward a rocky cliff a mile away. An instant later Lady followed. The rushing wind gave her a feeling of exhilaration and she reveled in the experience. Rapidly her speed reached eighty miles an hour as she approached the cliff. Dropping below the ledge she opened her wings and swooped up to land lightly beside her mate.

This was obviously a favorite perch of Patu and his former mate. The tops of the rock were white with the mutes of many years. For several minutes after the last rays of sun disappeared, the two eagles stood side by side in the cool air. Patu then made a short flight to a scrub pine that jutted out from the side of the cliff. Lady took up her roost spot in another pine a hundred yards away. As the hoot of great horned owls echoed across the canyons, Lady fluffed her feathers, drew one leg up and prepared to spend the first night of her new life in the wild.

chapter ii

At dawn Lady awoke and looked about. She stretched her right leg and wing down and away from her body and held it for several seconds. Then she repeated the action with her other side. She glanced over to the nearby pine and saw her mate preening. Her feathers began to fluff, giving her the impression of swelling. Then she roused vigorously, sending small bits of dust and body-down floating away. The air was still and she watched for several minutes as the white down drifted along the cliff.

The first rays of sun touched her gently and Lady looked back over her shoulder to the point on the cliff where she and her new mate had landed last evening. Presently she dropped from the perch, made a short circle out over the valley and with much flapping gained the rock. There she began to preen, in the regular morning ritual for golden eagles. Often an hour or two at the beginning of each day is devoted to caring for the feathers. The feathers of a bird of prey take a considerable beating during the course of the day. The large primaries beat up and down countless times a day and are forced to withstand tremendous forces in fast dives. Both tail and wing feathers literally are ripped apart as the bird breaks hard in a violent maneuver to catch prey. Often the most damage is done while the eagle is thrashing about on the ground, trying to subdue its prey. During these times the bird actually sits on its tail in order to allow free use of both feet.

With her powerful bill Lady began to work her feathers. The long primary wing feathers were usually first. Reaching back over her shoulder, she grasped a primary at its base and stripped it through her partially opened bill. This served a double purpose. Not only did it reposition the feather but as she pulled the feather through her bill she exhaled, thus steaming the thousands of tiny segments so they would zip together tightly. Every large feather received the same treatment. Then she began to work the smaller feathers on her breast, burrowing her head deep to get things straight. Frequently she reached over her back to the base of her tail where an oil gland is located. By pinching it lightly, a small amount of oil could be squeezed on her bill and worked into every feather, giving it a fine sheen. By now her black bill also was well oiled and polished to an ebony finish. Even her talons received attention as she fastidiously removed any fragments of dirt or flesh from them. After an hour of preening she straightened and roused again, ready for the day.

Glancing down the slope to Patu's roost she was surprised to see he was gone. Hardly had she noticed when she heard him calling from high above. As she watched with twisted head, he folded his wings and dropped like a missile. Reaching terminal velocity, he pulled out at eye level to Lady and shot upward, calling loudly. At the apogee of his pull-out he folded his wings until his body stalled and for a moment hung suspended in space. Then, tilting sharply over, he dived again.

Lady's excitement grew as she watched, and her vocalizations increased in proportion. Moments later she joined in the courtship activity. After mounting up, she tilted over and plunged downward, as if sliding down an invisible banister, and gained great speed. As she swept past her mate at more than a hundred miles an hour, she executed a half roll for his benefit. Her rolls were always to the left, never to the right. Perhaps, as in humans, eagles favor one side of their body over the other. On she descended down the canyon, splitting the air with her body and the silence with calls as she fell. Then along a slope where a current of air rose, she mounted up. This courtship activity lasted over an hour and in their exuberance both eagles had forgotten they were hungry.

The sight below of several ground squirrels in an open field reminded Lady of food and she began her stoop. It was a foolish attempt. The squirrels had long ago been alerted to the eagles' presence by the courtship activity. Long before she reached them, the squirrels had vanished into their holes.

Patu knew what would happen. From his experience he had learned that surprise was a critical factor. Lady's inexperience and overenthusiasm were a disadvantage as she tried several times that morning to capture prey. Meanwhile, Patu took a perch atop a nearby cliff where he had a commanding view of a small valley on the west side. In less than thirty minutes he launched and sliced down the hill, keeping close to the ground. As he crested a rise, three squirrels were surprised in the open twenty feet from their hole. With a

23

lightning move Patu was on one squirrel, crushing its life out almost instantly. Seconds later he mounted up with his prey dangling from his talons and returned to his perch.

Lady's repeated failures had tired and frustrated her. In disappointment she landed in a tall pine across the valley from Patu. Although over the years she had developed her skill at flying, she had had little experience in actual hunting, since her food had always been provided for her by humans. Now she would have to learn the skills of hunting from her mate just as a young eagle would learn from its parents. Searching the rimrock to the west she spotted Patu feeding on the squirrel. Immediately she launched and made her way across the valley. Minutes later she landed lightly beside him and eyed the food. Patu had eaten half, his appetite satiated somewhat, and he backed off, leaving Lady the remainder. Any other time of the year he might not have been so willing to give her his catch, but now it was spring and the male becomes more benevolent toward his mate. Eventually he provides all her food as she incubates. Lady consumed the food with relish, scrubbed her beak well on a twisted juniper root, and relaxed.

Although it is not possible for the mind of eagles to comprehend beauty and esthetics as humans do, they nevertheless are often found in the most spectacular country. The valley into which Patu had taken Lady was one of the most unspoiled pieces of country left in this populated part of California. It was nearly fifteen miles from the nearest road, that being only a country two-lane. Behind the valley to the north, rugged mountains and valleys extended for fifty miles with no signs of habitation. The same view spread out to the east.

There are several factors which influence an eagle pair to

accept a territory. A good supply of food and water is, of course, essential. Perches that give a commanding view and cliffs or trees that provide nest sites are just as important. In selecting this area, Patu and his former mate had done well. Not only did it provide all the necessities for eagles but, unknown to them, it was an area guarded from indiscriminate hunting by man. The territory consisted of almost all of the thirty thousand acres of the San Fernando Rey Ranch.

The original ranch dated back to 1846, when California was still under the flag of Mexico. Governor Pio Pico deeded thirty-five thousand acres of the Santa Ynez Valley to Nicholas Den. It was wild country then as Den journeyed up from Los Angeles to investigate his new property. He reported that it was doubtful if it would be of any use for cattle operations owing to the presence of numerous grizzly bears on the land.

Gone are the bears and now the ranch carries five thousand head of beef each year. Consequently no hunting is allowed on the property. The present manager, Gus Nash-Boulden, has been on the ranch for over thirty years, during which time he has developed a fondness for all forms of wildlife—predators included. For that reason no trapping or poisoning is allowed on the property. Even the ground squirrels, which on neighboring ranches are being poisoned, are not molested here. Gus is particularly fond of the large birds of prey and knows of most every red-tailed hawk's nest in the area. He has also observed that, for as long as he can remember, there have been golden eagles in the valley.

While Lady and Patu sunned on the rock, Lady had time to survey the country about her. In time she would learn every ledge and every hunting spot, but right now she was fascinated by the view of this valley that was to be her home.

The valley was shaped like a bowl, about five miles in diameter. Surrounded by lower hills on the southern fringe, and high mountains on the northern side, it provided wonderful slopes for updrafts and easy flying. The hillsides were covered in places with dense chaparral, which stems from the Spanish *chaparro*, meaning dwarf oak. Actually it is a dense thicket of several varieties of plants that have leathery, highly resinous leaves and extensive root systems that enable them to endure the dry seasons. In the center of the valley a small mountain protrudes up sharply. The slopes and flatlands are fine squirrel country, as Lady had already seen.

Running in a north-south direction, Peach Tree Creek wound its serpentine way across the valley. Tall cottonwoods, sycamores, and small willows almost completely hid the creek from view. Occasionally the lively sparkle of water could be seen between the green boughs. From time to time ducks visited the more open parts of the stream, pausing briefly on their way to Lake Cachuma, twenty miles to the southwest.

A slight breeze roused Lady from her idleness, sweeping upward past her and carrying with it a message—"Use me, fly on me, be swept to lofty heights on me." Of all flying creatures the eagle, more than any other, seems to be a part of the wind. They are truly born of the wind. A breeze can transform their flight from one of sluggishness and labored exertion to one of effortless, powerful flight.

With her feathers compressed tightly, Lady leaned into the wind, her wings slightly out, feeling the power in the breeze. Then she opened her wings gradually and leaned forward even more. Her feet became light and for a moment she teetered on the brink of the cliff, enjoying the anticipation of the metamorphosis that was about to take place. Then, with wings spread fully, she rose rapidly up and sliced along the rim of the cliff.

Patu watched with twisted head as she sailed back and forth above. By keeping her wings slightly closed, she reduced wing surface enough to maintain level flight, but upon opening them fully she ascended as if on an invisible elevator. Higher and higher she climbed until she was a thousand feet above the cliff. There, closing her wings, she hurtled down past her mate, calling loudly. He responded by taking to the air and joining her. Together they soared higher and higher, enjoying the command they had of the wind and the energies that the new season of spring stirred within them. Soon they were five thousand feet above the cliff and they could see over the coastal range of mountains to the Pacific and the Channel Islands beyond. It was a view befitting an eagle.

For thirty minutes they soared together, their circles entwining as they passed within a few feet of each other. Then, without a sound, Patu tipped over and plunged earthward. Lady watched while she made another turn and then she too plunged. Faster and faster they went, their speed exceeding a hundred and twenty miles an hour. Little wing surface was needed for control at this speed. Along their backs small feathers were sucked upward as a low-pressure area was created by the airfoil shape of their bodies.

Patu was not heading toward their perching site. Instead, he was aiming for the western rim of their valley, toward a group of cliffs. Gradually he leveled from the dive and headed for rimrock, executing courtship maneuvers. Nearing the cliff, he began calling loudly to Lady, who was not far behind. As he turned to circle, she sped past him, pulled up at a sharp angle, and landed on the rocky rim. But Patu had no intention of landing there. He wanted to attract Lady's attention to another spot on the cliff. This was one of the nest cliffs he had chosen for his previous mate, and now he was offering it to Lady. Several times he circled past her, calling excitedly, and then swooped down to land on the site a hundred feet below. There he walked to the jumbled pile of sticks and began to fuss over the nest, arranging twigs haphazardly. Several times he tried to coax Lady, with no success. After twenty minutes she followed him to the nest. She landed lightly on the edge and examined it closely while the excited male chirped in anxious tones.

But this had never been an eagle's nest. In some time past, a pair of ravens had apparently used it. The jumble of sticks was old but that could be improved. What bothered Lady, however, was the little protection from the elements and other predators. The ledge was on a steep slope and would be accessible to foxes and bobcats that could harm the eggs or eaglets. In addition, there was no cave or overhang for shade or protection from the wind. She examined the nest for fifteen minutes while Patu looked on anxiously, like a realtor trying to sell a piece of property. Then Lady took off. Sailing out over the valley, she gained altitude and headed for the high cliff perch. Patu looked for a moment, then joined her. His nest site had been rejected. It was her right to reject it, however, and it was his job to find another.

It happened that he had already located another site. For the same reasons that Lady had, his previous mate had also rejected the first site and although his pattern of offering it to Lady was still carried out, it was only by chance that he had chosen the rejected one to offer her first.

Later that day Lady caught her first prey, a brush rabbit

that appeared at the edge of the field below her perch. It was a thrill for her to experience for the first time the ultimate capture of prey. She rose easily on the wind with her prize and returned to the perch. Patu landed presently but made no attempt to take it from her. A few minutes later he stooped on a ground squirrel, missed, and finally settled for a gopher snake. He landed a quarter mile away from Lady and ate.

For the next several hours both birds remained on their respective perches. Around midafternoon Patu took to the air and coaxed Lady to follow him. This time he headed to a high ledge at the northern end of their valley. After diligent courtship and coaxing on Patu's part, Lady was lured to the second nest site. It was an old nest used several years before by another pair of eagles who had since vanished.

While Patu chirped encouragement, Lady hopped first to one side and then the other. For long minutes she studied the structure carefully and thoroughly, as if trying to decide whether it was worth remodeling. The structure was sound enough and there was protection from the elements. She began to express her approval with low chirps, which excited Patu even more. Then, as if to clinch the deal, she bent down and rearranged a twig. She accepted! Patu was delighted and dropped off the cliff to perform a series of acrobatics for his lady love.

For the next few weeks this cliff would be the center of their activities, but only another eagle would be aware of it, so secretive were they in their comings and goings. Patu became very domestic as he brought to the nest all sorts of twigs and sticks. Each flight was made in a manner to attract the least attention of anyone watching. From across the valley he would ring up with a twig clutched tightly in his talons. Casually he would drift in the direction of the nest but never coming closer than a half mile. Over a nearby hill he would soar, making a last-minute check of the country; then in a flash he would drop like a bomb below the hill and cut low across its slope, keeping well below the horizon. Traveling at high speed, he would hurtle down the narrow canyon that led to the base of the nest cliff. Abruptly pulling up, he would land beside Lady and present the chosen twig. Anyone watching would have had a difficult time tracking him. It was a natural precaution built into the eagle's behavior—a vestigial behavior pattern, perhaps, from an era when there were more natural predators threatening the eagles' nest sites. Today, with few natural predators, the behavior is still effective in protecting the eagle nest from the most mortal enemy of all—man.

Accepting Patu's offering, Lady fussed about the nest, looking for just the right place to put each twig. Patu's choices were thick twigs, half an inch or more, and provided reinforcement to the outside rim of the nest. A few moments later the two eagles dropped steeply off the nest and followed a winding canyon a half mile south before ringing up. Soon they found their way to their favorite perch on Goat Mountain.

From this spot they had a commanding view of the entire valley and a perfect view of their nest two miles away. Looking to the southwest they could see a segment of the highway fifteen miles away where occasional cars sped along. Frequently Lady's eyes were drawn to a spot on the oak-covered slopes of the coastal mountains. It was over twenty miles away, but still she could identify the spot. To the human eye aided with binoculars only a tiny splash of rust red might be visible, but to Lady's keen eyes it was the red tile roof of her former residence. It was coincidental that this territory her mate had taken her to was in full view of her former home.

During the first few weeks of her new life, Lady often glanced in the direction of the tile roof, and on a few occasions her sharp eyes recognized a figure walking about the point. There was never any desire to return to the place where she had lived with humans because she never really felt she had left. Her life now was only an extension of her former life, a new dimension. She still used the same landmarks for orientation that she had always used. There were even times when she soared the same slopes as she had when she was in captivity. The human companionship which she had enjoyed for so many years had been replaced by her wild mate. Although she had enjoyed the former situation, the bond with her mate was infinitely stronger.

The sound of pebbles tumbling down the mountainside startled Lady from her complacency. Looking back over her shoulder she saw, not more than a hundred feet away, two goats and a kid standing precariously on a steep slope. At first she was ready to fly, but her mate's unconcern reassured her and she watched with interest. She had never seen goats before, at least not that she could remember. The black billy, with his beard, looked impassively up at the two eagles, then jumped lightly across a small gully. The nanny followed, leaving the kid to bawl at his isolation. Soon he too clambered across the spot, kicking loose a small avalanche of rocks that tumbled five hundred feet down the cliff. Lady twisted her head and watched the rocks fall to the bottom. Her attention was then fixed on the goats as they made their way slowly up a hogback toward the eagles. They were incredibly slow, taking nearly an hour to cover fifty feet.

32

Theirs was a life of leisure. It wasn't uncommon for one to spend fifteen minutes between steps, just staring vacantly down into the valley.

Patu had seen these goats many times in the past. Actually there were several more around. They were domestic goats that Gus Nash-Boulden had released at the base of the mountains eight years before. Originally, he had released four nannies and one billy, but the billy was sterile and no kids had been produced. Then, just a year before, he had added another billy to the herd and three kids were produced this spring. In the eight years, the small herd had never left the slopes of this one small mountain. Gus, therefore, had christened it Goat Mountain.

While Patu stared off into the valley, Lady watched curiously as the goats fed on dry shrubs not more than fifteen feet away. The kid would have been easy prey for the eagles. But with so much smaller prey about, the temptation never surfaced. If, through man's interference, its natural prey of squirrels and rabbits were eliminated, the eagle might seriously consider making a meal of the goat kids. But as long as natural prey abounded, Lady and Patu would live in harmony with the goats, at times even seeming to enoy their presence on their mountain top.

chapter iii

Each day now Lady became more and more preoccupied with her nest. The larger construction was over and she was very interested in making the nest cup as soft as possible. On her flights she would look for soft grasses and tips of shrubs. Frequently she would skim over the tops of bushes and snatch bits of soft leaves without even slowing down, or she would land on the ground and pull tufts of grass up with her bill. These special items were added carefully to the nest.

Her appetite dissipated and she became very calm and docile. In her body, two eggs were forming and she felt heavy and awkward. The loss of appetite was nature's way of protecting her from her own normal feeding habits. If she were hungry, she would naturally attack prey and could cause damage to her eggs. So she patiently waited, nibbling very little on the offerings of food brought by Patu.

Much of the time was spent perching in favorite places. One of these was an old oak near the brow of a hill across the valley. The thick leaves provided shade from the sun and there was always something to watch. Small birds were busy coming and going and a pair of red-shafted flickers had a nest in a hollow limb that had long since broken and hung at a grotesque angle.

It was here in this favorite oak, on a warm spring afternoon, that Lady had her first encounter with humans since leaving her former home several weeks before. At first she heard a distant familiar sound—the sound of an automobile —but she was not alarmed. It had never meant danger to her before so why should it now? As the sound came closer she began to look about, curious as to its source. Had her mate been with her he would immediately have flown off and she would have followed. But Patu was several miles away, one of the few times they had been separated.

The sudden appearance of the orange-and-black jeep from around a bend a hundred yards away almost startled Lady into flying. But she soon regained her composure and watched the auto draw near.

The driver of the auto didn't see the large eagle in the tree until he was only two hundred feet away. Lady watched as the car stopped and the engine was cut. The driver watched incredulously as the big bird turned away, unconcerned with his presence. Then he slowly reached to the seat beside him and raised a pair of binoculars. Lady was so close that he hardly needed them.

Gus Nash-Boulden was on one of his regular trips, checking out the cattle and the range. He had never before been this close to a wild eagle. For several minutes he looked at Lady through the glasses and was struck by her complete

35

unconcern. He couldn't detect anything wrong; she didn't appear sick or wounded. Slowly he opened the car door and got out. She glanced his way but didn't seem the least bit alarmed. Gus had always admired eagles. After several minutes he concluded that there must be something wrong with the bird. Taking off his hat, he began to wave and shout. Only then did she take off and he could see clearly that there was nothing the matter with that eagle. He realized then that it must be a tame eagle and decided to make this information available to the Museum of Natural History in Santa Barbara on his next trip to town.

From across the valley Patu had watched the whole incident. As he saw the vehicle approach his mate he tensed. The memory of his previous mate's death at the hand of man had not dimmed and he fully expected his new mate to fall victim to this man. When he saw her fly away unharmed he took off and mounted up. He joined her over the valley and for an hour they soared thousands of feet above the hills, out of sight of Gus.

The courtship was reaching its zenith, with much display and nest-building. Constant arranging and rearranging of the continuous influx of materials kept Lady busy. Copulation occurred one morning after a spectacular display of flying by Patu. Several more times that day and the next the two birds mated. A day later, at evening, Lady laid the first egg, a white one with brown splotches. She stood by it, vocalizing loudly. The next day she laid another egg, this one all white. A few hours later she began to incubate.

Nature provides marvelously for its creatures and Lady's body had undergone many changes to prepare her for this time of the year. A brood patch on her breast had developed in the past few weeks. This is a spot where the down next to the skin disappears, leaving a bare patch. Blood vessels enlarge and surface in the skin, providing a source of warmth with which to incubate the eggs.

Even though Lady had been captive all her life, this was not her first nesting experience. In fact, she had nested every year for the past twelve years. However, in the past her eggs had always been infertile since she had no mate. Her human owner had usually replaced her eggs with the fertile eggs of a goose or a duck, and in spite of the differences between eagles and barnyard fowl, she had successfully raised these foster youngsters.

Even this very spring she had already laid two eggs in captivity and had set on them a few days before her mate lured her away. But with the strong stimulus of her mate's courtship activities, her glands had renewed their vitality and now she was in her second nesting. It is not uncommon for birds to lay a second set of eggs when one set is destroyed or removed by collectors early in the incubation period.

One wouldn't expect so large a bird as an eagle to be as inconspicuous as Lady was once she settled on the nest to incubate. Looking much like a mother hen, however, she lay flat and low, scarcely visible.

There is a striking difference between the male and the female eagle, the female being considerably larger than her mate. This is true of most raptors. It is called sexual dimorphism by biologists. There are several reasons why this disparity of sizes is important to birds of prey. In areas where pairs of birds are restricted to smaller areas and prey is scarce, this difference in size is invaluable since each mate adapts to the size prey it can handle. Whereas the female takes jackrabbits, the male may take ground squirrels. This way the territory can better support the two birds.

The reason why the female is the larger of the two is that it makes her the dominant one. If necessary, she can take food from the male by force to feed her youngsters. She is also more capable of defending the nest against enemies. The smaller size of the male dictates the size of his prey. Therefore, when he is supplying food for young eaglets he brings smaller prey, which are easier for the youngsters to handle. As the eaglets grow, so do their food requirements. It is then that both parents take to hunting to fill the demand.

Patu now took over the chore of supplying food for Lady as she incubated. Actually, he seldom came near the nest except to deliver the groceries. The chore of incubating the eggs fell almost entirely to Lady for the next thirty-eight days.

For a bird as active as an eagle, the chore of lying flat on its breast for hours on end is very tiresome. At approximately two-hour intervals Lady would rise, stand on the edge of the nest and stretch her stiff limbs. For ten minutes, seldom longer, she would preen and relax, then return to the eggs.

At about noon each day Patu would arrive at the nest and Lady would turn over the domestic chores to him for a brief time. While Lady enjoyed a short flight, Patu settled somewhat awkwardly on the fragile eggs. He was usually visibly relieved at Lady's return and wasted no time in giving her back her job.

The talons of the golden eagle are powerful weapons when used for capturing prey. But these same talons are handled with utmost caution around the eggs. As Lady approached the nest she would begin walking on her elbows, leaving her talons as limp as a blade of grass. If they accidentally touched the eggs, they brushed harmlessly past.

Before actually settling down she rearranged the eggs, rolling them to prevent the embryo from adhering to the inside shell. Then with her powerful bill she chopped and pulverized bits of grass within the nest cup, making it as soft as possible. Satisfied all was in order, she lowered herself on the eggs.

In the second week of incubation, she saw the orange-and-black jeep again in the valley below. A half mile from the nest site the jeep stopped. Patu, who was on Goat Mountain, took to the air and drifted off in a direction opposite the nest. But his decoy flight did not confuse the men in the jeep. Gus Nash-Boulden knew where the nest was and had been watching it for several weeks. This time he was not alone, however. With him was another man who was also keenly interested in the eagles. Walking from the jeep toward the nest cliff, the men began to climb a hill across the canyon in order to gain a better view of the nest.

Lady watched intently. She was not in the least alarmed but she was not as unconcerned about humans as she had been the first time she saw the jeep. In the brief time she had been free, she had already begun to revert to the wild state of her ancestors. Eons of the fear of man had been built into every gene of her being and now it was slowly emerging. But she would never be as wild as her mate; she would probably always tolerate humans at a closer distance than would Patu.

The men across the valley stopped and studied the cliff-side. From her position in the nest, Lady could see but not be seen. There was something very familiar about the man with Gus. She studied the figure intently and soon recognized it as the man with whom she had lived for sixteen years. Ed Durden had been contacted by Gus regarding the tame eagle in the oak.

There was no question that Lady knew the man but she wouldn't have initiated contact with him. Although one part of her recognized in him the human who had been kind to her, the other part recognized him only as man, and man was to be feared. Her place was in the wild now and nothing could change it. She watched with interest until the two men left an hour later.

It was four days later that Lady again heard a sound strange to this valley. From the west she saw a huge red-and-white bird approaching and emitting a sound like an auto, but louder. She watched as the small plane circled and neared the cliff. Several times it passed by quite close but she was not alarmed. It was strange, to be sure, but she knew it wasn't another eagle, and for some reason she didn't associate it with man either—it was a neutral object to her. Perhaps if she had lived in one of the states where men hunt eagles from planes, she would have been afraid of aircraft. But here there was nothing to fear.

As the plane glided past, she looked up curiously. She didn't notice the man in the cockpit. If she had, she would have recognized him as the same one who had appeared with the rancher four days before. Ed Durden had taken to the air in his plane in order to get a closer look at Lady. Since her departure he had been concerned for her welfare. The chance observation by the rancher had revealed to him the location of an eagle that was quite tame and in order to positively identify this eagle as Lady, he had to have a close look. Lady had two white feathers on her back that would be positive proof.

Although she didn't realize it, this red-and-white aircraft had played an important role in her early life. It was from this plane that Ed Durden had originally spotted Lady as a nestling sixteen years before. Equally absent from in her memory was the routine experience of riding in it—she had even anticipated the trips because they always took her to the desert where she could chase rabbits. While Lady had unique experiences for her species with man's machines, she was now as far removed from civilization's inventions as any wild eagle.

There were several more visits by the airplane. The last time she saw it she was standing on a nearby ledge, preening her feathers. She had just straightened a particularly stubborn white feather on her back when the plane arrived. As it neared she roused vigorously and the two white feathers were clearly visible. She couldn't have known, nor would she have understood, the joy that flooded Ed Durden at the sight of Lady on her nest. For several minutes the valley rang with the echoes of the engine after the plane had vanished into the distance. In the returning quiet Lady settled down once again.

Toward the fifth week of incubation Lady began to feel movements in the eggs beneath her. She often backed off the eggs and just stood looking down at them. On the thirty-seventh day the first egg began to pip. Within the shell the tiny eaglet was hard at work, chipping away his prison walls. With each movement, Lady became more excited. Before long the change from a nonbreathing embryo to an air-breathing chick was announced by small peeps, as tiny lungs filled with air and vocalization occurred for the first time.

In four hours the chick had completed cutting the wall and

41

lay exhausted in the half-opened shell. Lady bent over and gently nibbled the chick into movement until he was completely clear of the shell. As he struggled, Lady helped by picking off him small bits of shell. Finally he lay in a wet heap, limp as a jellyfish. Lady immediately lifted pieces of shell and discarded them over the cliff edge. The remains of the embryonic sac she consumed, to avoid attracting insects and animals. Then she settled on the precious chick and the remaining egg. A day later the other chick hatched and Lady's first family in the wild was complete.

At this early age the chicks were very helpless. Even small birds could be a danger to them, so Lady set closely on the nest, keeping the eaglets buried deep beneath her breast. For the first day they remained still and did not feed.

By the second day the eaglets had gained the necessary strength in their neck muscles to feed. Patu was as proud as Lady was and eagerly bent to the task of supplying food. A brush rabbit was their first meal. Lady tore off small bits of meat and held them in her beak, gently touching the eaglets on their bills. They responded by making wild passes at the pieces of meat with their own open bills. Weaving back and forth as they did, it was a wonder that they ever made contact. As they grew stronger their aim improved and soon they were accurately plucking tidbits of meat from Lady's bill.

Far off at the southern rim of the valley, a single horseman appeared over the ridge. Closely following the first was another, and then another. Soon the trail down the slope was dotted with a dozen horsemen, and still they came.

Lady paused in the feeding of her youngsters to study this new activity in the valley. For an hour the line of men and horses grew longer and longer. It was *Los Rancheros*

Visitadores, the Visiting Ranchers, making their annual week-long trek from the Santa Barbara Mission to the Santa Ynez Mission. An exclusive club, organized in 1929, the Rancheros now consist of over four hundred horsemen from all walks of life. Many are local people but a good number come from distant states and several foreign countries, to live for a week in the manner of the old Mexican rancheros.

To some it is an attempt to recapture the lost charm of a bygone era, when life was casual and friendships were real. To others it is a respite from the stuffy offices and dreary monotony of everyday life in the cities. Some of the horsemen rode easily and confidently in their saddles; others bounced and bobbed awkwardly. Those in the front half of the line were alert and conscious of their surroundings, but those that rode in the rear hardly knew where they were and clung as tightly to their saddle horns as they did to their bottles. Nevertheless, they were all enjoying themselves in their own special ways. The strange-looking parade passed half a mile from Lady's nest, then turned sharply west, to follow Santa Cruz Canyon to their camp for that night, two miles away.

The young eagles grew rapidly and within a week had more than doubled their size. They weren't the prettiest babies in the world. Their heads, and especially their eyes, seemed grotesquely large for their bodies. Their feet, too, were oversized and awkward. The eaglets were inactive most of the time, lying low in the nest. But in another few days Lady would be free from the nursery. The chicks would be left alone most of the day while the parents watched from distant perches.

chapter iv

Against a stiff breeze Lady mounted up with wings fully spread. Angling across the valley, she soon found an upsurge of air on the westerly slopes. Higher and higher she soared. The feel of wind beneath her wings and the emptiness of space below her was an exhilarating feeling she had missed during the long days of incubation. Her young were two weeks old now and were lying quietly in the nest. Frequently, as she soared, she glanced down at the nest. In sheer pleasure she would close her wings and allow her body to stall. For a moment the wind ceased as she hung motionless in space. Then it increased against her as she plunged earthward at terrific speed. Gradually she opened her wings and shot up at a steep angle, only to stall again and repeat the performance. Each time she performed the maneuver she purposely lost several hundred feet in altitude just for the thrill of descent. She headed east for two miles, dropping at ever steeper angles, until she was over Peach Tree Creek. There she pulled up several hundred feet above the meandering creek and circled several times. The sparkle of the waters could be seen through the dense cottonwoods.

Her long days of incubation over, Lady was left with a great desire to bathe. She was accustomed to bathing at least twice weekly and had missed it greatly these past five weeks.

With a spot selected, she dropped quickly toward an open area and landed on a huge boulder. From there she could see a hundred yards up and down the creek. For several minutes she surveyed the area before flying to a gravel bar where a small eddy created a pool. Once again she looked all about before proceeding. Into the water she waded, until she reached a depth of about six inches. Dipping her bill into the water and raising it up, she drank deeply. Then she began to bathe by dipping her head repeatedly beneath the surface and rising up to allow the water to spill over her back. With feathers fluffed to allow the water to penetrate, she squatted flat, thrashing with both wings, flushing water into every feather. This vigorous splashing went on for a full minute until a scolding kingfisher began to bombard her with lightning passes and loud cackling. A bit annoyed at being interrupted, Lady emerged from the stream. At the edge she shook herself violently, sending sparkling drops flying in every direction.

Back up on the boulder she drooped her wings and turned her back to the sun. The kingfisher still scolded her from a dead snag near his nest downstream. Lady watched, fascinated at the life about her. Of all birds, raptors seem to be the most observing. All manner of life interested her. A dragonfly, its blue wings flashing, hovered nearby looking for prey. A second later a yellow-and-black butterfly fluttered past and the speedy dragonfly scooped its quarry from mid-air. Head twisted, Lady watched the rapid flight of the predacious insect.

Before long a male costas hummingbird, its brilliant purple gorgets flashing in the sun, discovered her and began a tirade of scolding that took him from eye level to a hundred feet above the trees all in two seconds flat. After five minutes of vocal opposition to her presence, he zipped away.

Now that her feathers were getting dry, Lady began to preen. Frequently her bill would come up covered with a bit of down. A sharp shake of the head sent the down floating away, sparkling as it passed through shafts of light. Once again the male hummingbird appeared but this time his attention was diverted by the floating piece of fluff. Quickly he raced over, snatched the prize from mid-air and zoomed away with it to use it as nest material.

In the shallow water, Lady's attention was attracted by myriads of tadpoles dotting the stream bed. A movement to one side caught her attention as a giant water beetle crawled out from beneath a rock. His back was an inch in diameter and was covered with over a hundred eggs, laid and fastened there by the female. With this nursery firmly attached to his back, the male beetle had no choice but to go along with nature's plan. Now, somewhat encumbered by his burden, the beetle darted forward and snatched a tadpole in his powerful jaws. Retreating to the safety of his lair, the beetle leisurely consumed his prey.

Upstream a parting in the bushes caught Lady's attention as a while-tailed deer and its fawn stepped lightly to the water's edge and drank. The tranquillity of the scene was suddenly shattered by the explosion of a rifle shot a hundred yards away. The doe and her fawn bounded instantly into the brush. Lady burst explosively off the rock, scattering leaves as her powerful wings gulped the air.

From under the trees two men appeared. They cursed at having missed the deer and expressed surprise at the eagle they had flushed. They were poachers, who occasionally came in from neighboring national forest areas. Such people weren't above shooting a calf and hauling it away either. And there is no doubt that the eagle would have been their target had not the sound of the shots given them away.

Lady mounted up and rapidly put distance between herself and the hunters. The experience had frightened her and increased her ancestral fear of man. Even here, in this protected area, she was not entirely free of man's threatening presence. Three miles to the east she found her mate and together they mounted up and gained the safety of the northern edge of the valley. It was time to hunt and they planned to use the cliff perch to scan the fields below.

For half an hour they perched side by side, watching intently the activity below. They had learned to hunt together, although they didn't always work as a team. But there was an advantage in hunting together, because usually prey could be caught quicker and their babies could be fed sooner. It was normal for the eagles to make several attempts before making a kill. There were many tricks to catching ground squirrels, for example, but they did not always work. Needless to say, the ground squirrels in the valley became very alert and cautious if an eagle was seen in the vicinity.

On their lofty perch, Patu shifted his position slightly and watched the activity of a particular squirrel far out in the field below. He was quite far from his hole and there was a likely chance the eagles could intercept him before he made it home. Lady, too, saw the squirrel and watched. When Patu dropped off the cliff Lady waited a few seconds before following. She kept a space of a hundred yards behind her mate as the two sliced down the hill. The squirrel spotted Patu when he was still three hundred feet away but he held his position. The squirrel also had a trick or two. His plan was to wait until the last second and then run toward the eagle. If his timing was accurate, Patu would be unable to correct for the maneuver quickly enough.

For long seconds the squirrel watched the eagle approach. He couldn't see that Lady was following directly behind. Just as Patu was about to drop and had committed himself to a certain spot, the squirrel darted toward him, barely escaping the deadly talons. Before the squirrel realized it, however, he had dashed directly into Lady's talons; his life was crushed out instantly. Teamwork had paid off and Lady mounted up to return to the nest with her prey.

As the spring days wore on, the youngsters and their appetite grew in direct proportion to each other. Both parent birds were actively hunting at dawn, when animal life is busy. Most often squirrels and rabbits were the prey, but occasionally other kinds of prey found their way into the nest. Sometimes the food was better than others.

One particular morning, just after dawn, Lady launched from the nest and headed across the valley to a favorite perch. Just as she was about to land, her eye caught a movement among the oaks near the creek. Remembering the incident with the hunter, she was about to turn away when several animals moved out into the open. She stayed low on the horizon to avoid detection while she studied these strange animals. They were obviously a mother and five youngsters. The mother was quite a large animal, much too big for an eagle to handle. Lady had never seen wild pigs before. They looked peculiar with their chunky bodies, short legs, and curled tails. The old sow was pawing and rooting the leaf mulch, exposing acorns, grubs, and other insects for the piglets. They scurried about the sow, squealing excitedly in answer to her grunts.

Lady crossed behind a ridge and landed on a bluff directly behind the pigs. Then she watched quietly while they rooted about, moving further into the open with each minute. The piglets were about the size of jackrabbits but they stayed close to the sow. After ten minutes one piglet became very interested in tearing into a rotten root. Since he was the farthest removed from the sow, Lady selected him.

Like a shadow she sliced quietly down the hill, keeping close to the sage. The sow saw her when she was only twenty feet away and instantly charged. Lady reached the piglet the next instant, talons came down, and in one movement the squealing piglet was sailing out over the valley. Lady labored heavily with her prey. She had almost made a fatal mistake. The chunky piglet was far heavier than she had anticipated and she had almost been pulled down. The angry sow would surely have attacked her violently. But that day the eaglets dined well and Lady learned a valuable lesson about her weight-lifting ability.

Golden eagles are capable of capturing many kinds of prey, often animals that exceed their own weight several times. Lady was now as efficient a hunter as any eagle and she feared few animals. But it is surprising that eagles, like some humans, have certain aversions. Lady, for example, was a meticulous eater. There were certain parts of an animal that she refused to eat. There were also animals that she

found repulsive and downright frightening at times. She had no appetite whatsoever for snakes. If the snake was already dead she might consider it, but she had never touched a live, moving snake.

During her years of captivity Ed Durden had often given her dead snakes, but show her a live one and she would flee. The problem with snakes, as far as Lady was concerned, was that there was just too much of them to grab at one time.

She had often seen Patu catch snakes but she always discreetly kept her distance. It was inevitable that sooner or later she would have her first contact with the slender reptile.

One afternoon while she stood at the nest, watching her half-grown eaglets play with an old bone, her mate approached from a high elevation. It was obvious that he had come from afar and had been hunting. As he pitched down in a triumphant dive Lady could see that he had prey. Rapidly he closed the distance and to her horror she saw that he carried a snake. With a loud call he swooped up to land on the nest, extending his feet as he touched down. He was as proud as could be. Lady took one look at the decapitated but still squirming snake and catapulted off the nest in a flurry of feathers. Patu, somewhat perplexed, delivered the snake to the youngsters, who wasted no time in pouncing on it. It was late evening before Lady returned to the nest.

During the days, except for quick arrivals and departures of their parents, the eaglets were left alone. They were large enough now to tear up their own food and often fought over the prey. Frequently one eaglet is larger than the other and succeeds in taking the food from the weaker one. As a result, one eaglet often dies or is killed by the other. Lady's offspring, however, were about equal in size and both would survive to adulthood.

The midday sun of late spring usually found Lady sitting in a favorite old oak. It was one of several perches she used because it afforded an easy approach and take-off. The tree itself was an ancient oak, older than most in the area. Huge horizontal branches spread out, giving the tree a diameter of almost seventy feet. Cattle often paused beneath its low branches to scratch their backs. If cattle were there, Lady usually shied away. She just wasn't used to the close proximity of the huge beasts.

This day, however, there were no cattle present and Lady sailed easily in and landed. Soon she was relaxed with one huge leg stretched out and her foot doubled up into a gnarled fist. A spiny fence lizard, nearly eight inches long, peered at her with beady eyes from another branch. Lady watched his sporadic progress along the limb. Frequently he stopped to do a series of push-ups which interested Lady. This push-up movement is the lizard's way of identifying his territory to other lizards.

Along the branch he moved until he reached the crotch of the huge tree. Then he moved down and crawled out on an object protruding from the tree trunk. Obviously this was one of his territorial boundary markers because he again performed the push-up exercise.

The object on which the lizard performed was not a part of the tree. It was what remained of an ancient shotgun and had rested in this position for nearly a hundred years. In 1875 a holdup man had stopped the Santa Barbara–to–Santa Ynez stage on the winding San Marcos Road twenty miles south. The bandit had gotten away with the passengers' money as well as a thousand dollars' worth of hexagon gold slugs used as payment to a cattle rancher in Santa Ynez. Riding into the back country, he had selected this tree as a hiding spot for the loot. The tree was much younger and smaller then, but contained a hollow in the crotch. The outlaw rode to the tree, tossed the gold coin into the hollow, stuck the shotgun in, muzzle first, and rode away, fully expecting to return at a later date.

He never returned, and over the years the oak grew and engulfed its treasure, concealing it forever deep within its heart. Now all that remained was the rusted remains of the gun embedded deep in the wood. No one would ever know the secret.

The lizard scurried down the tree trunk and onto the ground, searching for insects. Moments later a roadrunner raced from the sage and caught the lizard in its strong beak. After beating it senseless against a rock, the roadrunner swallowed it headfirst, tail and all.

Lady watched the drama below with mild interest. She was drowsy in the midday calm. Her mate approached from the west and landed beside her. She chirped a welcome and together they spent the lazy afternoon.

chapter v

Down by the creek the kingfisher family had left their nest in the mud bank. The parents were in the process of schooling their five youngsters in the fine art of catching fish. While the young birds watched, the parent birds would catch a fish, beat it senseless, and drop it into a quiet part of the stream. At first the young kingfishers' aim wasn't very good but they were energetic. Time and again the inexperienced birds dived, only to miss even a dead fish. Little by little they improved and after two days they were catching live fish. Finally, after a week, they were catching their own prey almost as aptly as their parents.

On the cliff two miles to the west Lady's youngsters had reached almost full size. Daily they stood on the edge of the cliff and flapped their wings vigorously while clinging to the nest. As they grew braver they often released their hold and bounced lightly on the ledge while their powerful wings got the feel of the wind.

They had been well fed and cared for during their weeks of growing. It was a bit perplexing to them when Lady landed on a nearby ledge with prey and refused to come to the nest. It was time that they tried their wings, and if the parents continued to feed them at the nest, they would have little reason to fly. A day or two of fasting and they would have the motivation to try their wings.

After a few minutes Lady flew past the nest with the rabbit dangling temptingly. The eaglets saw it and chorused their eagerness, leaning far forward but never quite taking that one important step. Lady landed a half mile away and consumed the rabbit herself. The eaglets, now quiet, huddled against the cliff in the shade and waited for the next mealtime.

The rearing and training of her eaglets was to Lady an instinctive reaction. During her many years in captivity she had raised fowl which were not of her own kind; try as she did, she could never coax those domestic geese and ducks to fly. One would think that after so many years of failure she would not try again. But the inherent maternal drive within her refused to accept those failures—if she had reared flightless youngsters for a hundred years she would, no doubt, have followed the same pattern each year.

Somehow she sensed now that these youngsters were different from the others she had raised. From the very first, the eaglets had acted properly as far as their mother was concerned. They had remained helpless in the nest as they should, instead of running about as the more precocious young fowl had done. It was now time for her young eaglets to break the bonds of the nest.

For the next two days Lady and Patu coaxed, enticed, and even intimidated the youngsters to try their wings. And as their hunger grew, so did their boldness. At last the larger of the two leaped off the ledge in an effort to follow Lady. With wings flailing wildly, he careened off down the slope. Lady was instantly at his side, giving encouragement. Carefully she guided the eaglet to a somewhat shaky landing on an outcropping of the cliff face. There she left him to eat the prey she had provided as a reward and returned to the hunt.

Within another two days, both birds were in the air with their parents. Now began a period of extensive schooling, during which the eaglets had to learn all the tricks of survival. For several days they experienced how their wings could bear them aloft. Constantly hungry, they followed Lady closely. She led them along slopes where the winds could buoy them up. At first they were frightened at the feeling of the updrafts, but soon learned that these were essential to easy flying.

More than once, one or the other crossed a ridge, found himself in a downdraft and was forced to land quite unexpectedly. There were many high-speed tailwind landings by the two before they realized that turning into the wind could slow their ground speed.

Selecting perches is also a skill that the eaglets had to learn. Not just any spot will do. A clear approach and take-off path are essential. The eagle is a heavy bird with over six feet of wingspread and they must plan to allow clearance for these appendages. Trees present a problem to young birds. It is only by trial and error that they learn which branches will support their weight.

The older of Lady's youngsters learned, much to its dismay, that the tops of oak trees could not support its weight.

On about her third day after having left the nest, the female offspring attempted to land on the top of an oak. She was inept at landing anyway, so when she settled on the tree it was without much control. As her feet grasped a small, leafy branch it bent under her weight, frightening her into releasing her grip. As she tried to get into the air again, her wings only thrashed against the oak leaves. She fell heavily against the bough and hung motionless, wings outstretched, her body suspended between the leafy branches. The more she struggled the deeper she became entangled in the twigs and leaves. Frustrated and angry, the young eaglet thrashed and voiced her feelings in loud twitterings. Between struggles she lay panting and exhausted.

A mile to the east Lady had seen her youngster's plight. Now she pitched down and sliced across the valley, pulling up to circle over the oak. The sight of her mother above brought renewed strength to the young eagle and she began to thrash about vigorously.

In spite of her efforts to get to the top of the tree, she kept slipping through the branches until her feet came in contact with the solid feel of a sturdy limb. Gripping the branch firmly, she folded her wings. She was in the heart of the tree and the only way out was down. It was contrary to her nature to exit from the base of a tree. Once clear of the over-hanging branches, she flapped into the air, slightly the worse for wear but a much wiser eagle. Soon she joined Lady on a nearby cliff perch where the order of the day was to reorganize her feathers.

The insatiable appetite of the two young eagles kept both Lady and her mate busy. The presence of the two youngsters tagging along and calling loudly didn't help matters any. An important part of hunting is the element of surprise. With

58

these extra eagles in the air, it was very difficult to approach prey unnoticed.

By necessity, Lady turned to a slower, easier prey, one that could be captured regardless of the eaglets' presence. She had never before caught a snake. But now, with hungry youngsters beside her, annoying her with their constant calls, she thought seriously of a snake for the first time.

The field below abounded with ground squirrels that peered from the safety of their holes, having been prewarned by the eagles' presence. At the edge of the field, Lady spotted a gopher snake making its way through the tall grass. She watched it carefully. Within minutes the snake reached a point where it would have to cross a section of clear ground.

With one eaglet close on her tail, Lady made an approach to the prey. Swooping low over the sage, she dropped suddenly on the unwary reptile. She grasped the snake with both feet and bit quickly with her powerful bill behind its head. Although she had never killed a snake before, instinct told her exactly where to bite. But even with its spinal cord severed, the four-foot-long snake writhed and squirmed in her grasp. Lady flapped and bounced about for several seconds, then dropped the snake from ten feet in the air. The female eaglet, who had just arrived, immediately pounced on it. In her excitement, the young eagle battled the now lifeless reptile until every reflex movement had ceased. After mantling boastfully over her first prey, she consumed the snake.

Lady, meanwhile, mounted up and crossed the valley to a favorite spot where she easily caught a rabbit. She had no sooner returned to her perch than her other offspring, the male, arrived. With typical innocent rudeness, he snatched

59

Lady's prey right from under her beak and began to gulp it down. She did not retaliate but seemed to accept this as part of motherhood. There would be a time, not far off, when she would cease to be as obliging.

The eaglets were eager students. Over the next few weeks they tried enthusiastically to capture the elusive ground squirrels. Little by little they became more proficient. The female was first to taste of the success of the kill. It was a brush rabbit. The male began with smaller prey, his first being a pocket gopher that extended itself too far from its hole. But in spite of their newfound ability to catch prey, they still followed their parents, hoping for an easy meal.

Near the end of June, Lady shut off her eaglets' source of free food. She had spent the early part of the morning at the south end of the valley and had caught a large jackrabbit. While she was feeding, the male youngster circled overhead and dropped down for what he thought was a meal he could share. He walked over and was about to make a grab for the rabbit when Lady uttered an angry twittering and lashed out at him with her talons. He was startled and backed off a moment.

After eyeing her cautiously, he walked around to the other side. Perhaps she had made a mistake. Lady now faced him with head lowered and hackles raised. The eaglet was totally confused by his parent's behavior. Once more he tried to move in and was repelled by her angry response. Finally, in disappointment, he flew off.

From now on the family relationship would begin to cool. It was nature's way. This was not conscious premeditation on Lady's part. The hormones that had changed her into a protective mother hen were now becoming impotent and her

tolerance of other eagles in her territory was becoming less each day.

For the next several weeks, the immature eagles remained in the valley but they caught their own prey and were self-sufficient. Still they were tied to the parents by a slim bond which was not mutual. Although Lady now ignored her young, they often followed her around the valley out of habit.

On one particular breezy day in August, Lady mounted up to several thousand feet and began to cross the valley to the south. She simply felt the urge to wander to the edge of her territory and she hadn't been to the south for weeks because of nesting activity.

As she worked her way across the valley, one of her off-spring joined her. It was the female and out of habit she still occasionally gave the food call even though Lady no longer fed her. The two eagles crossed a small highway and approached a ridge on the coastal mountains. Above an over-grown firebreak, Lady turned and began to quarter back and forth along the slope, riding the updraft. This was familiar country to her. She had flown this slope many times before when she was living with humans.

As Lady worked the updraft her youngster too plied the currents. She was as good a flyer now as Lady was but could easily be identified as an immature eagle by the white band on her tail and white wing patches.

A quarter mile to the east, a movement in the oaks caught Lady's attention. She watched closely and recognized it as a human. There was a house almost hidden among the oaks. Something about the place looked very familiar. She quartered into the wind and allowed herself to drift toward the house. Then a second figure appeared out on the point. Lady was strangely attracted to having a closer look at the two men but she restrained herself and gained more altitude. Still her youngster followed her. At four hundred feet Lady allowed herself to drift even closer to the house. This was too close for the young eagle, however, and she veered away and out over the valley.

Irresistibly Lady was drawn closer to the point on which the two men stood. Although the ancestral fear of man had surfaced in her over the last few months, the sight of the familiar homestead below soothed her fear. Beneath her was the large cage that had been her eyrie for many years. Standing on the point, gazing skyward, were the two humans with whom she had had a close relationship during those years. The older man was the one whom she had allowed to fill the vacant place of a mate. The younger man was the son. Against him she had held a grudge for the full sixteen years. There was little doubt in the men's minds that this eagle was Lady. She passed directly over their heads at a low altitude and looked them over closely.

For several minutes she soared over the point, unable to truly understand the attraction. She would never have exposed herself so openly to other humans. The familiarity about the place was enjoyable to her and she lingered. Her nostalgic journey was interrupted then by the sight of Patu several miles across the valley. She veered away and hastened to join him.

Later that week Lady took the final step to cut the parental ties which kept her offspring in the valley. As the young female tried to join her flight one afternoon, Lady suddenly turned on the startled eagle and drove her relentlessly to the eastern edge of the territory. Once she broke off the attack, however, the youngster began to drift back toward Lady as if it had all been a mistake and now all was forgiven. Once again Lady unleashed a furious attack, which sent the young one fleeing eastward.

For several days this process was repeated with each youngster. Finally, late one afternoon, Lady drove them without mercy until they were past Paradise Camp, ten miles to the east. They were now out of Lady's territory and she pulled up to watch. Apparently they had gotten the message because they continued eastward, past Gilbraltar Dam. They would now become wanderers for several years until they matured and found their own mates.

In the late-afternoon sun Lady landed atop Goat Mountain. The valley was quiet again and her responsibilities as a mother were over for another year.

chapter vi

A golden glow appeared in the east, sharply outlining the mountains against the sky. In the dim light, the valley below was only a montage of dark purple shadows and misty outlines of oaks. Toward the south, ground fog lay quiet along the surface.

As the sun rose and the cool air was warmed, the fog in the distant valley began to rise and creep closer. Like a living thing the fluffy white mass probed up each canyon with curved ghostly fingers. Foot by foot it rose, the sections quietly meeting and rejoining to isolate a hilltop and make it an island in the white sea.

From the top of Goat Mountain, Lady watched all below. As the sun's rays reached her, she began to preen. Still the fog crept on. The entire valley now was one huge bowl of downy white. Only Goat Mountain protruded above the mist. Even it would soon succumb to the fog's relentless advance. Within minutes only the very tip where Lady stood was visible. Then in a whisk, it too vanished.

On her perch Lady was suddenly conscious of the warming rays of the sun being shut off. Cold enveloped her and she fluffed her feathers. Droplets of water condensed on each bud and twig and on Lady's sleek back, only to break loose and tumble down the well-oiled feathers and drop from the tips.

Alone in this quiet world, the great eagle stared vacantly into the mist. On the other side of the valley her mate had roosted the night. Had she not returned so late the night before, she would have joined him. Her complacency was interrupted by the sound of falling pebbles from somewhere in the whiteness below. She listened intently and heard it again. Then, apparently satisfied it was only the goats, she resumed her normal posture.

An hour later, with the sun's rays getting stronger, the fog began to melt off. Little by little Lady's world got brighter, until once again she was in the clear. She roused vigorously, sending sparkling droplets of water in every direction. Then for the next thirty minutes she preened.

On the oak slope directly across the valley, shafts of light were beginning to illuminate the shadows. A movement under the trees caught Lady's attention. It was the old sow pig with several nearly grown piglets. Probably the same family from which Lady had extracted a piglet months before. She made no move now. The piglets were far too heavy for her and she remembered the ferocity of the sow.

The pig family was rooting beneath the oaks, where a good crop of acorns was now falling. It was a good year for acorns and the pigs were indulging gluttonously. As they pawed and rooted the ground their snorts and grunts could be heard at a great distance. They ate not only the acorns but roots, grubs, and even small rodents which they flushed from the dry leaf mulch.

Thirty yards up the slope another movement caught Lady's eye. A tawny figure crouched behind a fallen oak. The cougar was sleek and obviously well fed. For several minutes the big cat watched the noisy activity of the pigs. She was in no hurry. There was no urgency. The prey would be an easy catch. With scarcely a sound the cat moved along the fallen tree to a better vantage point. At an opportune moment she crossed a clearing and positioned herself behind a huge lichen-covered rock, resuming the watch with only a twitch of her tail revealing her intent. Just as a house cat plays with a mouse, the big cougar was enjoying the anticipation of the kill. Carefully she gathered her powerful legs beneath her, tensed her muscles and readied herself for the dash to the prey. She knew the pigs were fast but planned on being there before they even knew she was around.

Unleashing the powerful springs in her legs, she burst from behind the rock. She had gone no further than twenty feet when squeals of alarm scattered the pigs in all directions, their plump bodies crashing into dense undergrowth. For a moment the cougar pulled up, confused. From another point of concealment a large male bobcat had made his attack, oblivious of the cougar's presence. Since the bobcat was closer, he had succeeded in pulling down a pig and was trying to drag it into a thicket. The cougar, having pursued the remainder of the pigs unsuccessfully, now turned her attention to the bobcat with his quarry.

The smaller cat wasn't going to give up his prey so easily. Snarling and spitting, the bobcat backed toward the thicket of manzanita, dragging the dead pig before him. The cougar snarled and swatted a few times but the bobcat succeeded in making a safe exit. Robbed of her prey, the cougar turned and disappeared over a hill.

Lady had watched the whole episode with keen interest. Now a slight breeze stirred her into life. She launched and sailed along the ridge, riding the upsurge of air several hundred feet. Across the valley she saw Patu soaring and joined him. Together they soared higher, enjoying the cool morning air.

To the north of the two eagles, beyond their territorial boundaries and off the San Fernando Rey Ranch, a lone white-tailed deer stepped cautiously into a small clearing and sniffed the breeze. He was a handsome buck with eight points. He had only paused a moment when a rifle shot rang out, shattering the stillness. The buck bounded off instantly, leaving the hunter wondering how he could have missed. It was the first day of the deer season and the hills around would soon be echoing with the shots of hunters.

The buck continued down the canyon at high speed, his heart pounding with fear. With a graceful bound he cleared a fence and only then did he slow down. His head reeled and he shook it, snorting loudly. The hunter hadn't missed. The shot had pierced the lungs of the animal and even now he was slowly dying. He plodded along at a slower pace, each breath getting more and more difficult. Strange gurgling sounds came from deep within his chest as he bled internally, slowly drowning in his own blood. His wild eyes took on a glassy stare as he stood unsteadily. There were no more shots; he was on the San Fernando Rey Ranch. But the safety of the ranch meant nothing to him now. He collapsed in a heap with bloody foam oozing from his nostrils and waited for death.

High above the valley Lady had heard the shot. From her height it echoed countless times before weakening. Although she didn't understand the sound, it frightened her. To Patu it meant danger. He had seen his previous mate fall and had heard a similar sound. Rapidly the two eagles drifted to the south end of the valley, away from the hunters.

Neither had eaten yet and now they began to search the ground below. Patu began to work a ridge while Lady headed toward Cachuma Lake. She hadn't hunted there before but had often watched from Goat Mountain.

Below her now were flat meadows of ripening oats, scattered with oak trees. She set her wings and assumed a shallow glide toward the lake. Ahead and below her she saw a figure standing in the oats. It was tall and she was curious. She pitched even lower and made an approach. The great blue heron stood almost four feet tall. With its long, sharp bill it was an expert at stabbing gophers and field mice.

As the eagle approached, the large heron took to the air, squawking loudly. Lady was startled to see that the heron was as large as herself. She gave it a low buzz and it turned to threaten her with its foot-long bill. She would have none of it and continued toward the lake.

Over a freshly plowed field Lady paused to circle. Warm air radiating from the dark earth created a thermal but she only needed a few hundred feet. Once at altitude she again turned toward the lake.

On the near shore, scattered along the bank and well up into the grassland, were several dozen coots. Their plump, black bodies bobbed as they fed on grasses and other vegetation. They were unthinking creatures to wander so far up the bank. Nearly every day red-tailed hawks or prairie falcons took one of their number and still they returned to the grassy slope. They are waterfowl and can fly quite fast but are slow getting into the air and are not very maneuverable.

Lady pitched down and gained speed. She had never caught a coot before but recognized their vulnerability and hastened to the attack. She was now only twenty feet high and a hundred yards away. Her speed was about sixty miles per hour. The coots saw her and all made a mad dash for the water. Their spindly legs were a blur and their wings beat a staccato sound. Some flew, others simply ran full speed, headlong into the water. The airborne ones dropped like bombs below the water surface and the water was white with foam as dozens of coots hurled themselves into its safety.

Those far up on the bank were, of course, the last to reach the water. There were several that Lady could have caught, it was so easy. As she swooped low over the stragglers she reached out with one leg and neatly plucked one while it was in midstride. It squirmed slightly and died quickly in her strong grip. She sailed out over the water and curved back toward the shore. Below her the wakes of the survivors quickly subsided. As she climbed for altitude, black heads bobbed on the surface to stare dumbly at the retreating eagle. Before she was out of sight they began to emerge out on the bank again. Their late comrade would never be missed.

High above the valley Lady set a course for a rocky crag a mile to the north. There she settled and leisurely plucked the coot, sending black feathers floating in the breeze. Across the canyon she saw Patu make a stoop on a jack-rabbit and miss. He was still hunting. He was a bit wary of going to the lake because of the motorboats that occasionally raced across the water. With her crop full, Lady relaxed.

She pulled up one gnarled fist and assumed a posture of contentment.

It was midday before she roused from her lassitude and became conscious of an ever-increasing sound coming up from the valley to the south. She watched curiously where a small column of dust rose from a canyon. Within minutes several horsemen appeared from around a bend. As they made their way up the dry trail, each hoof sent up a small explosion of dust which joined the others in a cloud only to be blown away in the stiff breeze.

It was time for the roundup. Lady had grown accustomed to seeing the cattle grazing on the hillsides and paid them no attention. The dozen men now making their way up the valley would spend the next several days rounding up several thousand head. The cowboys always started at northern boundaries of the ranch and hazed the cattle south to the lower areas where the huge corrals and loading chutes were located.

Today was their first day and they would be working right in and around Lady's valley. Within a few hours the cowboys had scoured the northern borders and had started any cattle in these areas moving down the hills. Lady watched in fascination as the usually inert cattle thundered down the slopes. One joined another until several dozen followed timeworn trails down the slopes.

Occasionally a couple of wild steers broke away and tried to make it into another canyon. With yells and whoops the cowboys raced to head them off. All this activity, while interesting, made Lady a bit nervous. Her mate had already climbed high above the valley and moved west. The noise and presence of so many humans racing erratically across the hills finally stirred her into action also.

She launched from the cliff and skirted along the bluff. Allowing herself to rise a hundred feet, she reversed her quarter direction. Again she rose a hundred feet and now made a complete circle, keeping within the boundaries of the updraft. By using the continued updraft along the slope she rose steadily. Near the top she angled for a low saddleback, intending to ride the slope breeze up the south side of the mountain. As she crossed the saddleback she was startled to see a horse not twenty feet away. The cowboy had dismounted momentarily and the sudden appearance of the eagle frightened the horse into bolting and running several hundred feet before stopping. The cowboy could only stare after the retreating eagle.

Within minutes Lady was above the mountain slope and continued to rise. The day was perfect for soaring. The warm air of Indian summer provided many thermals. She rose steadily two thousand, three thousand feet above the valley. The cowpuncher below was but a speck.

There was silence as she floated effortlessly upward. Each thermal, a giant bubble of warm air, carried her higher. As she soared, her wings were sensitive to the limits of the thermal. If she reached the fringes of its buoyancy she could immediately sense it and turn back into its effect. Far below, the cowboy on the hill remounted, after watching incredulously the speed with which the eagle had risen to such height. The process had taken only ten minutes. Still she rose.

At seven thousand feet she topped out of the thermal's effect. Now she drifted westward out over the flatlands of the Santa Ynez Valley. This was farm country, the ground below dotted with tiny houses and neat geometric patterns of various crops. It was near here that Patu's former mate had been killed. There was no danger to Lady, however. With the unaided human eye she could not be seen.

The air was very warm, even though she was so high. As she soared, by habit her head swiveled back and forth as she scanned the ground below. Frequently she shifted her eyes to the horizon and skyward, keeping an unconscious lookout for danger.

It was on one of these precautionary visual surveillances that she saw a huge bird approaching her from the northeast. It was approaching at fantastic speed and she had hardly completed a turn when the thing was upon her. The occupants of the small twin-engine aircraft stared in disbelief at the eagle as they swished past. Lady recovered from her evasive maneuver and resumed her normal altitude.

Suddenly there was a sharp bump, which she countered by pulling in her left wing and righting herself. Then a turbulent series of circular swirling currents grabbed her with an invisible hand and flung her about like a speck of dust. Her large wings could have suffered damage had she not pulled them in sharply and held them close. Now she plummeted straight down a thousand feet before pulling out. She was out of the airplane's prop wash and the air was calm again.

Almost unconsciously she became aware of strange white silvery strands suspended around her. They were balloon spiders, hundreds and hundreds of them, each floating from its own silken parachute. Balloon spiders are one of several species that spin delicate webs atop bushes. A whirlwind or strong gust pulls them loose and carries them thousands of feet aloft. Each spider clings tenaciously to its web as it drifts toward an unknown destination. Some travel hundreds of miles before becoming snagged on a bush. Others might

float far out to sea and be lost. Still others would be snatched from the air by insect-feeding birds.

Several of the spider webs were now snagging on Lady's wings. She tried shaking herself free of the sticky strands but only became more involved. Dozens more wrapped around her shoulders and face. She hated the feel of the stringy webs on her body and knew of only one way to get free of them. Like a bomb she dropped from the sky, the silken webs trailing her like banners.

Once on a convenient perch near the lake edge, she began a period of concentrated preening to rid herself of the mess. After doing her best with her bill, she flew to a nearby pool where she bathed vigorously, flushing out the remainder of the webs. After drinking deeply, she returned to the oak to dry. The hour was late and she soon located a more suitable tree in which to roost.

chapter vii

For an entire week the quiet routine in the valley had been disrupted. The cowboys had crisscrossed the hills and canyons a dozen times, looking for strays. Nearly all the cattle had been herded into the corrals, where, with much bellowing and crashing of heavy bodies against chute rails, they were forced into trucks. Truck after truck had ground its dusty way back toward the highway. The constant pulsating echoes of their engines had driven much of the wildlife to cover and into quieter places.

Lady and Patu had been affected also by the activity. Their hunting routines were interrupted. Where they could usually depend on an easy squirrel catch, they found nothing. The noise and excitement had driven the rodents underground for a spell. Bush rabbits were more than normally nervous and seldom ventured far from the thickets. It had been a lean week. Although three days without food was not unusual for eagles and caused them no hardship, Lady now felt the urge to feed more strongly than ever.

For most of the week she and Patu had kept to the higher hills, where steeper slopes and thicker chaparral made poor hunting. Now she rose up on the currents, intending to cross over the valley to the lake shore to take a coot. While playing the currents along the slopes, she saw with surprise another large bird soaring. Immediately recognizing that it wasn't another eagle, she was intrigued by its size. As she drew near she saw that the huge black bird was almost half again her size. In spite of its ten-foot wingspan, the stranger posed no threat to Lady. It was a California condor, one of fewer than fifty that exist in the world today.

At one time, the range of the condors extended throughout the western United States and along the coast to Oregon. Two hundred years ago they were numerous. One early Spanish explorer reported seeing a large flock of them feeding on the carcass of a huge whale that had washed up on the beach near Point Conception.

They are graceful birds in the air, almost entirely black with a white triangle on the underside of each wing. As Lady passed quietly by, she saw the ugly, naked, orange-colored head of the condor swivel and watch her with apathetic, beady eyes.

As scavengers, the condors must cover vast areas in search of dead prey. Their huge wings are able to gather in the slightest breeze and carry them easily along. The one now flying with Lady was almost a hundred miles from its habitual roosting place in the Sespe Wilderness Area to the east.

After ten minutes of soaring, the condor pitched down to the northwest while Lady remained in her position. As she watched, she saw that the giant bird was heading toward several other condors. This was a rare gathering in the valley.

Gliding effortlessly down the slope, the condor eyed the scene ahead carefully. In a small clearing on a knoll lay the carcass of a deer. It had been dead almost a week, the victim of the hunter who thought he had missed and had neglected to follow his prey.

Already, turkey vultures and ravens were tearing at the carcass. The condors' keen sight had spotted these smaller scavengers from a great distance. Although they are usually timid about approaching prey if no ravens are about it, the presence of the sharp-eyed ravens below assured them that there was no danger.

Being such large birds, condors have to plan their landing places carefully. In dead air and with a full crop, a condor is often unable to get airborne. Often prey goes unmolested because of the difficult location in which it lies.

This deer carcass, however, was in a good location, having an easy approach and a good downhill take-off. One by one the large birds dropped lower and lower. Then, with legs lowered to slow their airspeed, they sailed gracefully in and landed heavily near the carcass. There were nine condors, about one-fifth of the world population. As they landed, the vultures and ravens scattered temporarily. At first the condors stood about ten feet from the carcass and appeared to ignore it. Three of them had dusky-colored heads, showing that they were immature. Several preened their feathers, in no apparent hurry to feed. Their search was ended. There was no rush: the prey certainly wasn't going anywhere.

Within minutes the ravens had returned to the carcass but the turkey vultures were more timid with their giant cousins looking on. Presently one of the condors, an adult with wrinkled orange head, walked forward and scattered the ravens by jumping into their midst. With loud, raucous calls the ravens circled overhead. Soon five of the condors stood on the deer and began to tear and wrench the flesh from the body.

Although their feet are huge, they are not as strong as those of hawks and eagles and are used primarily for bracing as they pull at a carcass with their powerful bills. Inside their mouths are small barbs on the roof and on the tongue which provide a good grip with which to pull.

One raven, more bold than the others, landed a few feet away and scolded the condors. They ignored him. After delivering a few more insults, the raven bounced in and began to make wild grabs at portions of the deer. Still the condors ignored him. One by one, other bold ravens joined him and ultimately there were several ravens darting about the condors.

From her elevation, Lady had watched the whole scene intently. Never before had she seen such a gathering. The condors intrigued her and, even more, the deer. She recognized that the condors and ravens were feeding. This must be investigated.

Dropping down in a steep glide, she made her approach. The ravens were the first to see her and sounded the alarm as they took to the air. The vultures followed. With a swoosh Lady landed atop the deer. It was as if the condors didn't even exist. With a flurry the large scavengers exploded off the carcass, some to get airborne, others to run off a few feet and stare at the intruder. The ravens added to the confusion as they dived and scolded at this new intruder.

After surveying the situation for a minute, Lady sampled the venison. At intervals of several seconds, one of the ravens would buzz by her, coming within inches. Each time she responded by jutting her head toward him and raising her hackles. Hardly had she returned to eating when another of the pests would give her the same treatment.

The condors, meanwhile, stood like somber deacons in a quiet circle, waiting for the eagle to finish. Lady was less than pleased with the situation. The meat was not to her liking, and the ravens made it unbearable.

As she took to the air there were caws of triumph from the ravens. While most of them returned to the deer, three self-appointed protesters made repeated dives on Lady as she tried to gain altitude. They kept her so busy dodging their black bodies that she had difficulty in gaining elevation. Finally, two of the trio tired and hurried back to the deer.

One stubborn pest was enjoying himself so much that he remained on the job with joyful determination. This obnoxious raven was going to get the best of Lady yet. In her efforts to avoid the trio she had flown down the leeward slope of a ridge and was now caught in a downdraft. As she labored against it, the raven used his smaller size and greater maneuverability to drive her even lower. Each time he made a pass, she executed a roll in order to extend her talons toward him. In so doing, she would lose twenty feet of altitude. Although a raven isn't capable of hurting an eagle, they are an annoyance, just as gnats are to humans. Once again the raven zealously shouted insults and bore down on Lady. She was only a dozen feet above the ground and rapidly losing flying speed when the raven closed on her. As he reached her, she rolled again but when she recovered she was almost on the ground. Clipping a sage with her wing, she cartwheeled into the wild oats in a jumble of black feathers. Instantly the raven was at her again, diving and creating a racket that echoed from canyon to canyon. In every way possible he was telling the world that he had gotten the best of an eagle.

Lady straightened herself and called back a few insults of her own. The hackles at her neck rose. She was infuriated and humiliated. Angrily she began to run up the hill to the summit. She knew better than to try to fly on the down slope. As she ran in her swaggering stride, the raven never let up. By the time she reached the top she was furious.

She paused briefly and then launched into the wind. Instantly the raven was on her but she didn't flinch until she had gained altitude. With loud, nasty calls, and bravery born of victory, the raven again dived at the eagle. But this time it was different. Lady was in complete control of the air and was intensely agitated. She waited until the precise moment and rolled to an inverted position. Lashing out with one foot, she caught the raven squarely on his black breast. Her talons sank deep into his feathers. The raspy insults of the raven turned suddenly to squawks of terror which became weaker and weaker. By the time Lady landed on a nearby cliff, the taunting protester's life was over.

By the end of the week the valley was quiet again; the roundup was over. The men and the trucks had done their job and returned to their homes. With the settling of the dust, life returned to normal.

It was Indian summer with a full complement of dry air and tender, dry grass that crackled underfoot. Although officially it was autumn, there was no color change. Autumn comes late in the Santa Ynez Valley and when it does there is scarcely a visible difference.

Beneath the oaks in the valley deer lay in small quiet clusters, flicking their ears at the incessant gnats and deer flies. The oppressive heat even kept the ground squirrels in their holes where the temperature was thirty degrees cooler. They only appeared above ground in the early morning.

In the shade of a coastal sage a jackrabbit crouched with huge ears erect. A sliver of light striking the ear revealed an intricate network of blood vessels within the thin tissue. Perspiration evaporating from the ears cooled the rabbit's blood as it was pumped through the network of vessels.

Several turkey hens moved slowly through the oak grove, feeding on the abundant acorns. From time to time they flopped on the ground with wings half opened to allow circulation of air around their bodies. In the huge oak above, a great horned owl roosted in the shadows, its only movement the rapid pulsation of its throat as it panted. Its feathers were tightly compressed to eliminate any insulating dead air spaces which might preserve body heat.

The only active creatures were the acorn woodpeckers, seen as flashes of black and white as they made trip after trip to an old sycamore. With the acorn crop in full swing, the woodpeckers were busily engaged in their mysterious habit of drilling holes in the bark and stuffing acorns into them. The old sycamore had over twenty thousand nuts stored in its bark and still the woodpeckers worked.

The steady drone of a million unseen insects permeated the air, a phantom orchestra performing ceaseless tuning exercises. Even the usually active ravens perched in various trees with bills agape.

High up the slopes on the northern edge of the valley where a few pines clung to the cliffside was the midday retreat for Lady and Patu. On the shady side of two adjacent trees the two birds perched. Their feathers were compressed and their mouths were agape. From this spot they not only had an excellent view but were able to catch the slightest breeze. Only during the early morning or late afternoon hours did they fly. The heat made them listless. Even their appetite was gone. If a sufficient breeze came up in the late afternoon, they would climb high and soar until dark.

From time to time Lady looked down far below to the sparkling waters of Peach Tree Creek. She longed to stand in the water. During her years of captivity she had often spent hot days standing belly-deep in her bathing pool, allowing the cool water to draw the heat from her body. But no matter how inviting the creek looked, she wouldn't dare go down. She knew that it would be a difficult, laborious climb back to the pine in this hot, thin air. No, she would stay right where she was and endure.

Curiously she watched as a dust devil whirled its erratic course across the flatlands three miles away, its siphoning effect lifting all sorts of debris hundreds and even thousands of feet into the air. At the top, where its effect was lost, the bits of leaves and grass were tossed out to fall leisurely back to earth.

By midafternoon a slight breeze began to stir. But it wasn't from the ocean; it came from the east, a hot, dry breeze. And it only increased the heat. Gradually the breeze grew into wind, the wind into a gale. This was the annual wind from the east, which whips into this part of California every autumn. Originating in the hot, high deserts, it moves westward and drops in elevation several thousand feet where it compresses and becomes superheated. By the time it reaches the coast it often has a velocity of sixty miles per hour and a temperature of well over a hundred degrees. The people call it a Santa Ana wind. The Forest Service calls it the devil wind.

In the flatlands below, the deer aroused from their inactivity. With noses lifted they tested this new wind. It brought with it strong scents from parts of the surrounding area that were foreign to them. The heat and extreme dryness of the air stung their nostrils. Several snorted. With the new wind came a restlessness for all wildlife. For the deer it meant that their noses and ears were not reliable. The noise associated with the gale would drown out any sound of danger. Almost in unison they rose and looked about nervously. They began to form a closer group.

In the tall grass horned larks huddled close to the ground and continued to search for insects. Frequently they rose vertically above the grass, their tiny wings beating furiously, and allowed the wind to move them ten feet. Then they dropped back down.

A gray fox, awakened from his sleep beneath a log, moved out into the field. Although not a hunter by day, the wind made him nervous and he prowled to ease the tension. It was purely by accident that he came upon the lark. With the constant movement of the grasses the bird was not aware of the fox until it was pinned beneath the fox's front paws. A quick bite on the lark's head ended its life.

Far to the east, about twenty miles away in a small canyon, was a dry campground. Typical of campgrounds in this region, the place had a few tables, some fire pits, and no water. Situated amidst dry chaparral, with loose sand about, it was no place to be in the heat. A lone camper, an unlucky deer hunter, packed his belongings and hastened to move out of the campsite. As his pickup hurried down the road, it was enveloped in a cloud of dust. He was glad to be on his way.

Because he had no water, the hunter had covered his campfire from the night before with several inches of sand. He even piled rocks on top. He had been careful, but not careful enough. The relentless force of the wind pried at the sand covering, grain by grain. Within two hours most of the sand was blown away. Only the heavier rocks remained to hold down the charcoal-blackened pieces of wood.

Deep within a blackened chunk of wood an ember still glowed, and the wind reached down and brought it to a deep red glow. Within minutes a particle of red broke off and was blown across the sand, to become lodged against a rock where it died, harmlessly. But more particles followed, some to perish, some to live. One lodged between the dried roots of a creosote bush and a small wisp of smoke rose to be swept away by the wind. Suddenly the ember burst into flame and the flame hungrily fed on the bush. In moments the entire bush was on fire and bits of flaming bark were being hurled to other bushes.

In the dry country the fire spread quickly. The wind and the low humidity only added to its fury. Within ten minutes a column of white smoke rose ominously into the sky. The fire lookout on La Cumbre Peak spotted the telltale sign and the alarm was given.

From her lofty perch Lady could see the column of smoke. It did not concern her. To her it was only a small cloud. But the devil wind was working its magical powers on her as well as the rest of the wildlife. With nervous energy she rose against the wind and climbed rapidly. Patu followed. For several thousand feet they rose vertically, playing the wind to its fullest, taming its wild energy into usable forces. Although they were now five thousand feet above the valley, the column of smoke to the east was above them. As the hot air rose, it created its own wind effect, adding to the holocaust below.

From several directions vehicles with lights flashing hurried to the scene. A Forest Service helicopter throbbed its way across the valley. Lady had never seen a helicopter before and the peculiar flashing of its shiny rotors frightened her. She gave it a wide berth.

For an hour and a half the two eagles soared almost invisibly above the valley. Then, from the direction of the coast, a great silvery bird appeared over the ridge. It was well below the eagles and they watched it with interest. The vintage B-24 bomber was hurrying to make one of the first of many aerial drops of fire-retardant chemical solution. The eagles watched as the huge plane flew low and dropped its load of liquid. There was a brief lull in the flames but soon they resumed their fury. It was evening before Lady and Patu returned to the cliffside. They found a sheltered cove on the northeast side and settled for a fitful night's sleep.

Throughout the night the fire raged unchecked. The dry chaparral, full of volatile sap, literally exploded as the intensely hot air reached it. Hordes of wildlife fled before the flames. Some were lucky to be fleet of foot enough to outdistance the flames. Others simply went below ground and were protected in the cool womb of the earth. Still others succumbed to the flames. Of those that fled, both predator and prey ran together in a temporary alliance necessitated by the common threat.

With the dawn, an unreal sight greeted the eagles. The

cloud of smoke was now dark gray as the fire consumed heavier brush and oaks. It hung like a huge umbrella over the entire area, fifteen thousand feet overhead and filtering out all but the orange and red rays of the sun. The sun itself was dimly visible as a blood-red balloon. The wind, which had died a little during the night, now began to pick up. Lady noticed a white covering over the rocks on which she stood. The fine ash had sifted also into every crevice of Patu's and her own bodies. She shook herself and sent a shower of ash flying. After preening a bit, she looked around. She didn't like the situation at all. It was weird. Although she had just awakened, it felt like evening.

With the eerie light of dawn, sorties of water bombers thundered across the valley. Smaller bird-dog aircraft buzzed about, directing the larger aircraft. Bulldozers and other heavy equipment growled their way slowly up the fire roads. In the valley below herds of deer stood in frightened clusters, unable to understand this threat.

Many smaller animals had found refuge in the valley. It would have been easy hunting, but Lady was too nervous about the situation. Besides, her appetite was still dulled because of the oppressive heat.

Presently, as if by mutual consent, both birds mounted up. They gained altitude rapidly and with a purpose. This valley was not its usual self. The presence of so much activity and the approaching fire influenced them to seek more serene areas. Under normal conditions they would never leave their established territory. Ever higher they climbed until they could clear McKinley Mountain. Then they headed northwest at a fast ground speed with the devil wind at their backs.

chapter viii

The northern portion of Santa Barbara County is rugged country. It is mountainous, with heavy chaparral on the lower slopes, oaks in the canyons, and pines on the higher slopes. Except for an occasional fire road, there were no signs of civilization.

As Lady and Patu reached a point nearly twenty miles north of their home territory, they suddenly realized they were no longer being pushed by the devil wind. They had reached the limits of its effect. The thick, impenetrable smoke canopy no longer blocked out the sun. Once again the sky was blue and the air smelled clean. Both birds began to soar on gentle currents, relieved at last to be away from the wind and fire.

They were not alone. Several other raptors had fled the fire and were also enjoying the clean air. It was cool and re-freshing. After days of the oppressive heat Lady suddenly felt alive again. A turkey vulture passed by several hundred feet below and, in a moment of devilishness, she stooped on it. Several times she dived on the distraught vulture, coming within inches but never striking it. It was only play on the part of Lady, a way to vent her exhilaration.

Soaring on the same currents as Lady and Patu were several red-tailed hawks and one Cooper's hawk. Lady had seen the small Cooper's hawk in her valley before, but never had she seen it up so high. It was a swift, maneuverable raptor, very apt at darting through trees in pursuit of small birds. The smoke had forced the Cooper's hawk to leave the valley also and now he soared along with the eagles, looking like a miniature replica of the larger birds.

As the odd assortment of raptors reached a point over a broad valley, they broke up. The red-tailed hawks dropped down to a lower altitude, where they began to scan the ground for pocket gophers and other small rodents. The vultures soared along the ridges on their never-ending search for carrion. The Cooper's hawk headed for the thickly wooded north slope of the valley. As he neared the oaks he suddenly turned and darted into the trees, twisting and turning as he streaked between gnarled trunks. Bursts of feathers marked his progress as juncos, towhees, and jays scattered in all directions to flee the hawk. In seconds he stooped upon a surprised towhee that had become too engrossed in scratching out an insect to hear the sounds of alarm shrieked by the other birds. Moments later the Cooper's hawk swooped up to an oak to consume his prey.

Lady had seen the entire chase from above. The reckless speed with which the Cooper's hawk had hurled himself through the trees fascinated her. She recognized that he had prey and her own hunger became noticeable. She began to scan the ground below, her sharp eyes probing into every likely spot.

She was still several thousand feet above the valley, far too high to make a surprise attack on anything. Although she knew this, she lingered at this altitude, enjoying the commanding view. Patu had, by now, dropped to a lower altitude where he quartered back and forth along a ridge, ready to drop on an unwary rabbit. In moments he stooped with success on a cottontail.

Lady was about to descend and begin serious hunting when something up ahead caught her attention. At first she was intrigued by the flock of large birds flying a precise V formation. She had never seen Canada geese before. In fact, they were not frequently seen in Southern California. The flyway was a hundred miles to the east, where refuges in the San Joaquin Valley attracted thousands of the geese to winter. Occasionally a small flock somehow found its way further west. They were on a direct course for Lake Cachuma, which was only thirty miles south. They would probably spend several months there, feeding in the nearby grain fields.

A steady fifty miles an hour was their speed as they constantly conversed in their mellow tones. Their V pattern, which is so esthetically pleasing to humans, is a very functional part of their flying. Each goose benefits by the one in front as the air flows over the forward bird's back. Consequently, all but the lead bird have easy flying as a result of this effect. The position of leader is constantly changing as the flight progresses, in order to distribute the burden of being at the front.

The skein of geese passed over the northern rim of the valley just a few hundred feet high. One more ridge and they could begin the long descent to the lake. It would be easy going from then on.

From her lofty position Lady studied the flock. She was two thousand feet above them and they would soon be passing directly below her. Although she had never seen a flock of Canada geese before, she was not entirely a novice to goose hunting. Years before, she had caught a white domestic goose while she was flying freely outside her cage. The human who cared for her had not intentionally launched her at the goose; it was just by accident that the flock had flown and she had reacted instinctively. Their size was about the size of the Canada geese below. She knew she could handle one and the challenge of new prey, coupled with her hunger, was overpowering.

She let the flock continue a bit until they were slightly south of her. Then she pulled in her wings, tipped down, and began to plummet earthward. In moments she was moving at a hundred miles an hour. She singled out a trailing gander on the right side of the V.

The eagle was still a thousand feet above them when the geese spotted her. They all headed instinctively toward the ground, even though there wasn't a body of water for miles. At her speed of over a hundred and fifty miles per hour, Lady rapidly overtook the flock. The trailing gander was trying desperately to put on extra speed but to no avail. Lady slammed into his heavy body with tremendous force. Her speed had been so great that she had only hit him with half-opened talons. As she pulled up steeply to check her speed, she looked down to see that the gander had straightened out and was continuing somewhat shakily on course.

Once more her wings closed and she dropped. This time she locked tightly to him with all talons. With wings out-

stretched, both birds cartwheeled to the ground. Even before they reached the ground the goose was dead, a quick death with little pain. The cartwheeling mass of feathers landed heavily on a grassy slope. The spot didn't suit Lady well, since it was directly beneath a rock ledge. With much tugging and flapping, she was able to get atop the ledge with her prize. Soon the feathers were flying as she plucked the goose.

Her appetite satisfied, she was in high spirits. An hour later Patu arrived. Lady, by now, had gorged to the fullest and was willing to let him sample her catch. Although he had just eaten, the taste of wild goose led Patu to gorge himself further. For several hours that afternoon the two birds remained side by side on the ledge, letting the heaviness of the meal wear off.

Toward evening they began to arouse from their gluttonous stupor. Lady saw a movement below and watched as a small red weasel darted from under the ledge, grabbed a scrap of meat, and dashed back. A breeze stirred and sent feathers from the goose dancing off down the slope. She launched into the wind, climbed up to the top of the ridge, and settled in an oak. Soon Patu joined her and the two prepared for the night.

For several days the two birds wandered around this new territory. To Patu, this was familiar country—the territory he had shared with his former mate. Now it was unoccupied. On more than one occasion, however, they saw other eagles. The first encounter was one afternoon as they soared several hundred feet above the ridge, enjoying the lift. Lady was startled to see above her another eagle. Immediately she began to climb for altitude. If the other bird was hostile, she was in a poor position to defend herself. As she climbed she saw that it was an immature male, one with much white on his tail and wings. He had no intention of being hostile, for he, too, was a wanderer, not because of the fire, but because he hadn't as yet selected a mate and established a territory. Like Lady's youngsters of that spring, this eagle would wander for perhaps four years before settling down. Lady soon recognized that the stranger had no territorial claims and the two soared together for thirty minutes before he drifted away to continue his wandering.

The sudden appearance, a few days later, of a mature female eagle sent a shudder of fear through Lady. In her own territory she never knew the feeling of fear, but since arriving in this valley she had been a bit apprehensive. Although she had carefully looked the area over and had found no eagle occupants, she nonetheless was never completely at ease in this unfamiliar area.

The encounter this time occurred when both birds were low to the ground. Lady had just taken off from her morning perch and was in the process of finding a thermal over the valley when the other eagle appeared suddenly over a ridge. Both instantly saw each other and began to protect themselves by gaining altitude. As they soared in tight circles a half mile apart, each bird watched the other for some signs of territorial ownership. Although Lady didn't know, the other female, too, had been displaced by the fire. Now each expected the other to declare ownership by a significant flight pattern.

Territorial defending is very strong in eagles and usually the intruding eagle does not stick around to fight. At this moment Lady was ready to flee at the slightest indication of ownership on the part of the other bird. She knew it wasn't her territory. For the same reason the other bird was ready to flee.

For a half hour the two birds soared, each cautious about the other. There was no need to fight. There was no territory to defend. They were on common ground and, like two opposing warriors meeting in No Man's Land, a truce was declared. They tolerated each other's presence. For the next two days the other female hunted the valley, never joining Lady and Patu, but not avoiding them either.

Twenty miles to the southeast the massive fire was almost contained. Over two thousand professional fire fighters struggled to contain one last hot spot along the forty-mile front. In the accessible valleys untouched by the fire, support crews worked to supply the tired men with meals and their vehicles with fuel. Everywhere trucks, helicopters, and other equipment were busy with the battle.

It had been a bad ten days for the wildlife of the area. Those that could flee did, but many were trapped by the flames. Most birds were able to keep ahead of the fire, although there were always those who waited too late to leave the cover of the chaparral and became incinerated as the volatile brush exploded.

There were also those who benefited by the fire. Already ravens and vultures were returning to the burned-over areas to begin their grisly role in nature of consuming the bodies of the victims. By some miracle there were even a few surface animals, such as rabbits, that had managed to survive. As soon as the earth cooled, ground squirrels began reappearing at the entrance to their burrows to stare in wonderment at the change in the landscape. The dry grasses of summer had all been consumed, leaving only a white ash. Sage, madrone, manzanita, and ceanothus all were only naked, blackened skeletons of their former shapes. The rank odor of burned brush stung the squirrels' nostrils and many of them retreated to their burrows.

On the twelfth day of the fire the last spark was snuffed out. The last shovel was thrown into the last truck and the army of men and equipment ground their dusty way back to the highway. The toll had been great. Over forty thousand acres of valuable watershed had been destroyed. Countless animals and birds had met death. The cost in dollars was staggering, but it was over. The fire had been contained just on the fringes of the valley in which Lady and Patu lived.

chapter ix

Although smoke billows were no longer visible on the horizon to the south, Lady and Patu still lingered in their new territory. Perhaps it was the refreshing change of landscape that held them, just as people often seek new surroundings. Whatever the reason, it was intangible to either of the two eagles. They knew only that it pleased them for now. The fact that it was unoccupied eagle territory was, of course, the deciding factor. As long as it pleased them, they could remain in this new area.

As the days wore on, the two eagles found themselves returning habitually to favorite perches. One of their favorite hunting spots was a flat tabletop of land called Hurricane Deck. Jackrabbits abounded. The Sisquoc River flowed along the eastern slopes of the deck and tumbled westward toward the Pacific.

There were no signs of civilization in sight. This was the

San Rafael Wilderness Area of the Los Padres National Forest. This 145,000 acres was the first addition to the National Wilderness Preservation System as provided by the Wilderness Act of 1964. According to the Act's definition of "Wilderness" it is . . . "an area where the earth and its community of life are untrammeled by man, where man himself is a visitor who does not remain." True to its definition, the area was free of man's presence. Only a few hiking trails and primitive campsites existed. During the dry summer season not even these few trails are in use, since the area is closed because of high fire hazard.

High atop White Ledge Ridge, Lady sunned herself. The late October air was cool and the warming rays of the sun felt good. Although it had been autumn for several weeks, this was the first day it had felt like fall. The air was saturated with floating seeds, as many plants dispatched their various fruits to the dispersal of the wind.

Far down below her, Lady could see the sparkling waters of Sisquoc River as it worked its way west. Along its banks sycamores and willows provided habitat for many forms of wildlife. Oregon juncos, down from the North, scratched in the loose loam for insects. An American goldfinch, already in its dull olive green winter plumage, landed on a small rock, drank twice, and returned to the willows.

A hundred yards downstream, the river widened and slowed as it rounded a rocky promontory. Here sedges and cattails grew in the shallows. The cattails, which had sported such well-groomed velvet heads all summer, now looked disheveled as the heads burst. Each head looked as if unseen hands had plucked the velvet surface as a child, in curiosity, will pluck the stuffing from a pillow. Countless seeds floated away on the wind to search for habitable niches.

Some seed clumps landed on the quiet water to set sail for a distant shore.

The lower portion of the cattail stalks was ringed with white marks, indicating the various water levels in the river from the high of early spring to the present low of late autumn. On many stalks the dried skeletons of the spring crop of dragonfly nymphs remained fastened. The young dragonflies had emerged to seek their way of life as one of nature's fastest-flying insects.

Although thousands of the predacious dragonflies had emerged, only a dozen still hovered above the pond. As they hovered, inches above the still water, their long abdomens curved down. With a quick dipping motion, the tip of the abdomen ejected egg after egg into the water. The tiny crystal spheres floated to the bottom to lie in the mud until spring. The journey to the bottom was precarious and many eggs were snapped up by mosquito fish before they reached the mud.

The activity of the dragonflies was watched by a sharp-eyed kingfisher sitting on an old snag above the pond. From previous experience he knew that the dragonflies often attracted the small fish. With a flash of white wing patches, the kingfisher dived headlong into the water. An instant later he burst from the water with a two-inch fish. With a loud cackle he landed on the snag, neatly flipped the fish into a headfirst position, and swallowed it all in one motion. Shaking himself dry, he resumed watching the stream surface with alert eyes.

A slight breeze began to stir as the sun-warmed earth radiated heat. Lower layers of air were in turn heated and rose up the slope toward Lady. Having finished her morning toilet, she cast off and rose on the lift. Since she had fed late the day before, she was not searching for food. Rather, like so many others, it was a flight born of the moment, for no particular reason. The spirit moved her to fly and she did. This freedom to mount up at the slightest whim was still a joy to her. Although she had been free for six months now, she hadn't learned to take this freedom for granted. There was an intangible, subconscious awareness of her new life that pleased her.

It is difficult for humans to accurately describe the behavior of animals without using human descriptive terms. We can describe what we see, but often the visible action is quite different from the true or real behavior. Consequently, most nature writers tread softly lest they fall into the dreaded anthropomorphic pit.

To say that Lady appreciated her new life would be to imply that she had the ability to compare the two worlds she had lived in and arrive at a conclusion that this one was better. Let us say, rather, that the pleasant things of this life, the exhilaration of truly free flight, the vastness of her domain, and the daily challenge of survival created in her an eagerness to live that had just recently awakened. Just as young eagles thrill to the breaking of their bonds to the nest on their first flight, so Lady felt now. Although sixteen years old and fully matured, she was really a juvenile in her first year of life's experiences.

As the wind pressed against her outstretched wings, her body rose effortlessly to a thousand feet above the valley. The brisk autumn air was invigorating and for some unknown reason she felt a bit devilish. Perhaps it was a combination of the cool air and her youthful zest for life that caused her to search for something to bedevil. A quick scan of the sky revealed only a raven, far too quick for her to harass. But she would have welcomed his scolding at the moment. She searched the ground below for signs of life. There were several ground squirrels in the field and one jackrabbit sitting beneath a shrub. But these were her natural prey. It had to be something exciting. Perhaps even a bit dangerous.

Along the edge of a clearing she saw a shadowy figure creeping ever so slowly. She watched the coyote as he carefully stalked a ground squirrel. He must have had an unsuccessful night's hunt, because normally he would not have appeared in daylight. Lady watched in fascination as the large animal calculated his chances. Suddenly he burst from the brush and dashed for the unwary squirrel twenty yards away. The squirrel surprised him by ducking down a convenient hole. Irritated and puzzled, the coyote sniffed at the hole and whined and pawed a few times. He was so engrossed in his vanished meal that he didn't notice the dark speck in the sky that was rapidly increasing in size.

From her vantage point Lady had watched the coyote begin to dig at the hole. With his back turned to her, he was completely preoccupied with the squirrel. It was a perfect set-up. If one was going to heckle, the element of surprise was half the fun. In years past, she had often taken great delight in badgering various dogs that passed near the property where she lived. This often caused great distress in her human master but she never harmed the large animals. Usually a few close passes were enough to send them yelping for their homes.

She was now a quarter mile away, about five hundred feet high and moving fast. Her fast glide was punctuated frequently by well-placed wingbeats. She looked determined and ominous. Anyone watching would have been certain that she was determined to grapple to the death with the coyote. Even while in flight the golden hackles along her neck were raised. But this was all part of the game—just as a cat, with twitching tail, will carefully stalk a rubber mouse. In spite of these outward signs, Lady had no intention of making contact.

The coyote's nose was still in the squirrel hole when there was a tremendous roar as the diving eagle pulled up inches above his back. The accompanying dust, wind, and dark shadow startled him beyond all reasoning. His first reaction was to whirl to protect his exposed rear. But there was nothing there. For an instant he was puzzled. At that moment the eagle had reached the top of her pull-up and, with a sharply executed wingover, was now plummeting toward the coyote's backside again. This time he detected her a split second before her pull-up. With snapping jaws he jumped toward her and bit down hard on empty air. She was already fifty feet above him.

Leveling off, she orbited above him, flapping hard to maintain slow flight speed. For several seconds the coyote snapped and growled at his lofty tormentor. Then, realizing it was futile, he made a dash for the sage. As soon as he turned, Lady made another pass, causing him to whirl and snap again. Several times she stooped on the distraught animal before he finally made it to the safety of the sage.

Lady was in high spirits. It had been an exciting experience. Although it had all been done in fun, there was a valuable lesson learned. The coyote was not to be dealt with lightly. She now knew the speed with which he could react and the danger of his jaws. Most behavior patterns in nature have a function, and this play session was very important to the eagle. Just as the cat develops its skills on the rubber

103

mouse, so the eagle develops its skills even in play. Should the time ever come when she would find it necessary to attack a coyote, this play session would be invaluable.

She was still in a playful mood; perhaps it was even more intense because of the coyote experience. She set her wings and soared close along a bluff where a stand of yucca grew. The only green part of the plants was the sharp swordlike spears that radiated out from the base of the stalk. The dried stalk, about three inches in diameter, was over six feet high. On top were the dried seed pods which, in spring, had been such beautiful white flowers. As Lady skimmed over the yucca she dropped her feet slightly and grasped a fistful of seed pods, then dropped them to rattle down the slope. Each time she drifted over the stalk she repeated the act, as if it were done unconsciously, much the same as a boy, walking through a field of wild oats, will strip off the dead seeds through his fingers.

After five minutes she landed on a lichen-covered rock. The rock was rough and pitted. Centuries of red and green lichens had slowly crumbled the rock, reducing it back to the soil. She looked about, alert and eager. Her feathers were still compressed tightly, evidence that she was not yet ready to relax.

Something behind and to her left caught her attention momentarily, but she looked quickly away. She cocked her head skyward, whirled and, with lightning speed, was on the ground, grappling with the twisted root of a long-dead juniper. Again and again she gave the old wood death-dealing blows and squeezes. Using her wings to balance herself, she hopped about the ground with the root in her grasp. Once or twice she dropped it from a few feet in the air and pounced on it furiously. Finally she managed to get it to the edge of a slope where it bounced downhill, much to her delight. It had hardly stopped bouncing before she was on it again.

This play had a two-fold purpose. While it was idle entertainment, it served a more useful function as displacement activity—behavior that exists in most higher forms of animal life, including man, as a vent for frustrations and anxieties which build up from outside stimuli.

In Lady's case, what had started out as play with the coyote developed into something a bit more. Her natural instinct to grapple with the coyote had increased as the play progressed. But she was not yet ready for such combat. Now that the play was over, she felt the need to express her aggressiveness on even an inanimate object. The old root sufficed and for a time she dealt it every death blow she knew. Oftentimes birds or animals will repeat functions such as preening or scratching over and over in order to expend nervous energy. This form of diverted activity is shared by man. Witness the child who, in response to his mother's punishment, will pinch his baby sister. Or the adult who smokes cigarette after cigarette while waiting for a job interview.

After five minutes of vigorous play, during which time she had fairly well swept the bluff clean with her huge wings, Lady hopped back up on the rock. In moments her feathers rose violently, sending dust and debris flying from her body. Her nervous energy expended and her eyes sparkling, she began to preen her feathers.

On the ground below her, in a small hole not more than an inch in diameter, four black, beady eyes emerged to stare fixedly at Lady. The interesting thing about these four eyes was that they were all attached in a lateral line to the same

head. The slight movement caught Lady's attention and she watched with interest as a black, furry body emerged from the hole. The wonder of it all was that the tarantula spider was at least three times the diameter of the hole.

In her thrashing about, Lady's wings had apparently removed the protective web that the spider spins across its hole before retiring before dawn. Now he would have to replace the damage in broad daylight. Lady watched as the large spider folded its legs and somehow squeezed into the hole headfirst. In seconds, tiny spinnerettes on his abdomen began to spin another door across the hole. In less than a minute the hole exterior was very effectively closed and the spider was protected from its natural enemies.

Later that day Lady took a jackrabbit and fed high atop the bluff. By the time the meal had worn off it was late in the afternoon and she elected to stay there for the night rather than seek out her mate.

chapter x

From an elevation of five thousand feet, the view to the east from the bluff was spectacular. It was midmorning and the waters of the Sisquoc River shimmered in the distance. The eye could follow its serpentine course past Cliff Canyon, Rattlesnake Canyon, to the south of Samon Peak, and finally to its source on Big Pine Mountain, some seven thousand feet high. Perhaps the most beautiful spot on the river is at Sisquoc Falls, where cascades fall some two hundred feet down sheer cliffs into a wooded canyon. Manzanita, madrone, oak, and many forms of hard and soft chaparral cover the canyon walls, and the river flows into several smooth, rocky sections where shallow pools form.

This canyon lies in the heart of the Sisquoc Condor Sanctuary, twelve hundred acres set aside for the condors' roosting and nesting sites. On a white ledge a few feet above a pool, an immature condor with naked gray head ponders, in its dull way, whether to bathe or not. It looks cautiously about and is a bit nervous. Nothing is more helpless than a soggy wet condor. It bends down and picks up a twig with its beak and then drops it, a displacement activity to soothe its anxiety. Finally, satisfied all is safe, it enters the pool. A moment later it is joined by another condor who, secure in the presence of the first, enters the water immediately.

From her elevated position, Lady has seen the condors bathing and is stimulated to bathe herself. She pulls in her wings and begins a long, gentle glide to the water.

The eagle's eyes are not the only eyes that have been watching the condors. The tawny form of a cougar is barely visible from within the cave in which he had been sleeping. The sound of the condors landing had awakened the sleeping cat and now he watches with growing interest. Little by little, he creeps to the mouth of his lair and studies the scene below. The condors are standing in the center of the pool about fifteen feet below the ledge on which the cougar stands. He recognizes that these birds are no more dangerous than a wild turkey he once caught. Their clumsy, shuffling walk indicates to the cougar that here is a prey not too quick on its feet. He moves closer to the edge of the ledge, under cover of heavy chaparral.

Before the cougar can make his move, there is a sudden flurry of wings as the condors frantically flap their soggy way out of the pool and up on a rock. The cougar is about to leap when another flurry of wings stops him cold—Lady has landed at the pool.

While the condors eye her nervously, she proceeds to bathe vigorously in the cold water. The cougar recognizes instinctively that the eagle is a bird of prey and one he has no intention of attacking. Quietly he slinks back into his den.

It was good that his attack was thwarted. The condors below represented one twenty-fifth of the world's condor population. Had one of the young birds perished, the species would have been dealt a severe blow.

For an hour Lady dried in the sun while the condors dried themselves fifty feet away. A breeze came up and the vultures launched heavily into the wind and soared gracefully out over the valley. Hunch-shouldered and clumsy, in flight they became creatures of beauty, a rare metamorphosis. In a clearing below, two rutting white-tailed buck deer paused in their combat to look up at the two condors. The condors paid them no attention whatsoever, since the deer were living and they dealt only with death.

From her drying rock Lady had an excellent view downstream. The water tumbled down a series of steps and flowed out into a flat stretch with sandy banks. In the crotch of a low overhanging oak a furry ball slept the day hours away. Were it not for the bushy tail which, at the moment, concealed the eyes and nose, one would have had difficulty identifying the animal. Although its color blended perfectly with the gnarled oak bark, the black bands on its tail were a dead giveaway. The young male raccoon slept peacefully, with only an occasional convulsive jerk as his subconscious mind thwarted an enemy.

During one of these convulsive moves, the tip of the tail slipped from its appointed spot and dangled in the breeze. Further muscle spasms, as well as the breeze, caused the tail tip to move in quite a rhythmic pattern. It was this tempting target that drew the attention of a scrub jay, that self-appointed guardian of the wilderness. It is this fellow who takes as his sole duty in life the responsibility to warn his fellow citizens of anything that seems amiss in the environment. Had the raccoon's tail not dropped, the scrub jay wouldn't have given him a second glance. He had long ago spotted the sleeping animal, but a sleeping raccoon is of little danger. Now, however, the peculiar, unnatural movement of the tail brought the jay to his finest hour. In seconds he launched into a tirade at the tail and began orbiting the tree while shouting obscenities at the raccoon.

The pointed ears of the raccoon twitched slightly as they read this new sound. Unconsciously his mind was constantly reading sounds from the woods and he was expert at sorting out the important from the ordinary. If he jumped to his feet every time he heard a jay scold, he would never sleep. The woods were constantly bombarded by the jays scolding one thing or another. So now, the jay's shouts were dismissed.

Back and forth, around and around the jay flew, from the top of the tree to the stream's edge, constantly rasping out his doomsday warning of the strange creature in the oak. With each tirade he grew bolder, landing on closer branches, then darting swiftly back to a safe distance. He was doing a fine job, for now several other birds arrived to see what was up. Spurred on by an audience, the jay became blurry flashes of blue as he grew bolder and bolder in his obsession.

Little by little the noise was beginning to wake the raccoon. At first he laid his ears back, as if trying to shut out the infernal racket. Just as he was about to gain consciousness, the jay dashed by in a daring maneuver and lashed out at the tail with his sharp bill. There was a sudden lurch as the raccoon came to life. The jay flashed by with his booty, a beakful of raccoon fur. Instantly the raccoon was atop the

111

branch, fur bristling, back arched, and head lowered for battle. The heroic jay, now beside himself with the success of his attack, was joined by others. With the mob of jays flashing about him, the annoyed raccoon begrudgingly gave up his lofty perch. The jays didn't let up until he was a hundred yards upstream, galloping through the shallow water.

Once peace was restored, the raccoon meandered along the stream bank. Although he seldom looked down, his soft velvet paws were constantly searching the stream for interesting things. Idly he brought up a stone and turned it over and over in his dexterous hands, feeling its smooth contours. Moments later he discovered a hole and, while gazing blankly into the distance, rammed his left arm down to his armpit, but came up with nothing. Still constantly searching, he overturned a rock and discovered a large water beetle, already sluggish with the dormancy of coming winter. The raccoon's sharp teeth crunched the shell and the beetle became his midday snack.

Bit by bit, pool by pool, the raccoon worked his way upstream. Lady hadn't moved from her drying rock and had watched his progress with growing interest. His seeming preoccupation with his work gave the impression that he was unaware of his surroundings. It was while he was engrossed in extracting a frog from beneath a moss-covered rock that Lady launched. She gained speed fast as she glided silently down the slope toward the unsuspecting raccoon.

If there is one creature in nature that is able to rally in a crisis and gain control, it is probably the raccoon. Nature has provided him with keen reflexes and extremely fast movements. He is built low to the ground and, as a result, has a low center of gravity. His four velvet-clad paws give him excellent traction as well as claws with which to defend himself or climb a tree. Razor-sharp teeth are his main weapon and it is said that he can shred a hound dog to pieces in a fair fight. His entire body is sheathed in a tough skin clothed with thick fur. When engaged in battle, every hair rises, almost doubling his size and giving him quite a fearsome appearance.

The element of surprise would have been complete had it not been for the angle of the sun. The late-autumn sun, low in the southern sky, was at Lady's back. Consequently, her shadow preceded her a split second. This slight warning was enough to change the odds in the attack. Lady had been approaching over the raccoon's right shoulder and had intended hitting him directly on the back of the head with one taloned foot and on his shoulder with the other. Had she been successful, she would have had a kill.

Owing to the shadow's warning, however, the raccoon whirled with incredible speed and met her talons with open jaws. This sudden turn of events startled her into making a split-second abortion of the attack. However, the raccoon's reflexes were so fast that he lashed out at her foot as it passed inches above his head. Lady was conscious of a sudden pain in her foot as she pulled up sharply to avoid colliding with an oak branch. As she turned at the top of the pull-up to begin another dive, the raccoon was ready. His size had nearly doubled, his back was arched and his head was low. He was prepared for any attacker foolish enough to try. Lady's initial attempt at surprise had failed and she had no intention of pressing the attack further. In a face-saving gesture, she stooped on him again but pulled up safely out of reach of his jaws. The raccoon snorted and snapped at empty air and began a backward retreat toward the trees. He had nothing more to worry about. Lady had learned a

hard lesson. The raccoon is not an animal easily captured; many an immature eagle has met death during its first year by foolishly grappling with one.

Lady skirted the eastern canyon slope where the west wind was deflected up and rode the elevator to a thousand feet. The pain in her right foot had turned to a dull throbbing. She wanted to put a good distance between her and the canyon, so she headed west to familiar country. After an hour she spotted Patu, who also was soaring. As she neared him, he joined her. His crop was bulging from a recent meal and he no doubt was looking for a good perch on which to spend the afternoon.

Although Lady hadn't eaten all day, she had no appetite now. She pitched down and headed for a rocky cliff above Hurricane Deck. Patu followed and soon the two perched side by side. Lady didn't realize the extent of her pain until she tried to stand on the injured foot. Immediately she drew it up and looked curiously down. The palm of the yellow foot was ripped open, a deep gash about an inch long. The yellow-scaled skin was already puffy. Blood still oozed from the wound. Already her body was reacting to the injury and she felt sick and weak. Unlike mammals, who can lick and cleanse wounds, the eagle can do nothing. Since their feet are their weapons with which to catch food, an injury to a foot can often cause a slow, lingering death by starvation.

For the rest of the afternoon Lady rested, standing on her good foot. Toward evening she took a perch in a nearby tree and spent the night in fitful sleep. The next two days were a haze. In some mysterious way she knew that she was in danger of falling off a tree perch, so she spent all her time on a rocky ledge, alternately standing on the good foot and lying down. A fever raged throughout her body as infection

115

set in. She grew very thirsty and the fire within her compelled her to seek water.

Patu, sensing something was wrong, had stayed near and now followed Lady as she glided down to the river. Instinctively she sought a place open and free of predator cover. In her weakened condition she was in no shape to fight off a coyote or a bobcat.

She landed heavily on her good foot at the water's edge. After glancing about, she waded directly into the cold water. The cold felt good to her swollen foot and she drank deeply. The water began to work its magic and in minutes the fire within her began to cool. Several times she ducked her head under and raised it up to let the water run in glistening drops down her back.

Lady stood nearly immobile in the pool for several hours. Her eyes were dull and she scarcely looked about. Unconsciously she knew that the less energy she expended, the better her chances of survival. Her mate, perching nearby, gave her a feeling of security. Toward midday she hopped up to a nearby rock and lay down. Several times that afternoon she awoke and reentered the water to drink and soak.

It had been nearly five days since she had eaten. During that time the fever had killed her appetite and she hadn't even noticed the absence of food. But now the infection was diminishing and the fever was leaving. Her body was weak from the experience and the lack of food was telling.

For three days she stayed near the river, drinking and soaking during the day and spending the nights atop a handy boulder. On the third day she saw Patu dropping down from high altitude with a cottontail dangling beneath him. She watched hungrily as he landed on the bluff and began to feed. Unconsciously little chirps emanated from within her breast and a clear liquid began to flow from her nares (nostrils). Ten minutes passed and she could stand no more. She launched from her rock perch and laboriously worked her way along the east bank until she had altitude to reach Patu. Upon landing, she uttered the feed call again, one which she had seldom used since leaving the nest. Patu recognized her desire to feed and made no attempt to mantle (conceal with his wings) over his prey. She moved in, hopping on the good foot, and lashing out rudely for the rabbit with the injured one. Pain stabbed through her foot and leg but she ignored it and began to feed. Frantically, she ripped off large chunks and bolted them down. Within minutes only the rabbit's feet and head remained. Lady stood with crop extended, her hunger satisfied. Only then did Patu move in and nibble at a few scraps. Even he didn't understand his benevolence. It was nature's way, an advantage of being mated for life. Lady would have done the same thing for him without understanding.

It was several more days before she resumed normal flying. Her strength had returned but her foot was still a real problem. The swelling in the palm wouldn't go down. Each toe was fattened to the extent that she couldn't close the talons. Although the infection was gone, a tiny burr within the now nearly closed gash was causing problems. The burr had been squeezed into the open wound as she landed on a rock minutes after the bout with the raccoon. Now the flesh was festering, as nature tried to isolate the intruder and wash it away.

For a week or more Patu willingly gave up his catch. But now that she was flying normally he was less agreeable. Lady was forced to feed on the remains of his catch and, consequently, was never completely satisfied. Sooner or later

117

she would have to resume hunting, but she felt inadequate to tackle normal prey. It was this feeling of insecurity in her ability to handle prey that drew her inexorably back to her nesting territory. After an absence of six weeks they were headed homeward. They didn't go straight to their destination but spent several days in a circular route, swinging in a wide arc to the west.

They passed over rolling, oak-studded hills where cattle and horses grazed leisurely, westward over Zaca Peak, and across Sisquoc Valley. This was historic country below. It was down this valley that General Frémont, with a few hundred whites and some Walla Walla Indians, made his way in December of 1846. The war for California's independence from Mexico was in progress and Frémont was headed south to engage the Mexicans in battle at Santa Barbara. A few miles south, the Mexican *comandante* waited in ambush at Gaviota Pass. But Frémont, suspecting such an ambush, turned east along an Indian trail and, with tremendous effort, managed to move his entire force over San Marcos Pass and take Santa Barbara without a shot. The war for independence was over.

Twenty miles ahead, Lady could see the old Indian trail, now a paved highway. Several times she had stooped on prey but had only been successful in capturing a few pocket gophers. The handicap of the injured foot forced her to seek easier prey. The memory of the coots on the banks of Lake Cachuma and the ease with which she had caught them was a compelling force to return to the familiar valley.

The two eagles were now flying high over cultivated land, fields of sun-ripened grain and alfalfa. Ranch houses stood on the foothill slopes and there were many cattle. It was in similar country that Patu had lost his previous mate. He was

118

reluctant to descend to a lower altitude. But Lady dropped lower to scan the pockmarked hills for game.

Since it was late autumn, most ground squirrels were in their burrows, but in this mild climate usually a few remained active all winter. Along a south slope, near the edge of a cleared field, Lady spotted a likely prey. The squirrel was far from a hole, wandering about in apparent unconcern for predators. Several times he stumbled and staggered and there was an appearance of helplessness in his movements. Lady recognized his abnormal behavior. Here was easy prey. She pitched down and circled around to come in low over a knoll. Still the squirrel acted strange, at times falling and rolling on the ground. If Lady had not been handicapped, perhaps she would have avoided an attack.

But she was moving fast now, very low and due to sweep over the knoll in seconds. Suddenly, a gray figure burst from the nearby brush and in one bound snatched the squirrel practically from Lady's talons. The bobcat was as startled to see Lady as she was to see him. She pulled up abruptly as the cat bounded off into the brush with his prize.

It was bad luck for the moment but it saved Lady's life. The bobcat was even now consuming the body of the squirrel, a body which was saturated with poison placed by a local rancher to kill squirrels. The poison, called 1080, is a lethal compound which is not biodegradable. It had been killing the squirrel, and would now kill the bobcat, and then whatever fed on the bobcat's carcass. Finally the poison would leach into the soil itself where grass roots would absorb it, ultimately finding its sinister way into the bellies of the very cattle the rancher was trying to protect from squirrel competition. Before the day's end the bobcat was dead. And the irony of it all was that the rancher, in an attempt to control the squirrel population, had instead killed one of the most efficient squirrel predators in nature.

For Lady it was an opportunity missed. She had no way of knowing of her close brush with death. She rose up on the currents and rejoined Patu and together they soared away from the lethal ranchland below. Ahead and to the southeast was the shimmering blue of Lake Cachuma, the western fringe of their home territory. After six weeks, they were returning to familiar places. A tingle of excitement ran through both of them as they came closer.

chapter xi

In the clear autumn air the crisp outline of the distant mountains rose majestically skyward. In the sparkling waters of the lake, shallower by twenty feet because of the long, dry summer, schools of huge gold carp could be seen here and there from the bluffs high above.

From this vantage point, a lone rider paused to look at the school of gold carp before continuing on his chores. The cowboy breathed deeply of the clean air and was about to press on when his attention was attracted skyward. With squinted eyes he followed the two eagles as they crossed the sky two thousand feet above. Past Johnson Canyon they angled down. To his seasoned eyes the eagles looked as if they had just returned from a morning's flight. Nothing indicated that they were returning from an absence of several weeks, that they were coming home.

As the eagles neared Boot Canyon, Lady veered south and

dropped a thousand feet before leveling. The cowboy watched the huge bird drop even lower and just barely skim over the ridge at the foot of Middle Canyon. Then it sliced toward the lakeshore where a flock of coots lounged peacefully on the bank. In a flurry of black bodies the coots scattered and for a moment the eagle was lost in the confusion. Seconds later she emerged out of the flock at high speed with a coot tucked neatly beneath her. The cowboy whistled softly at the precision with which the eagle had executed the attack. For Lady, it was precision born of necessity. She hadn't even touched the ground; her injured foot had not been used. With the speed she now attained, she was easily able to gain the windward slope of a hill, where she mounted up and soon was lost to view.

For the next few days her foot swelled and festered, as the burr worked its way toward the surface. It was quite by accident that the problem was solved. Upon returning from a flight, she had to extend her swollen foot to steady herself against a gust of wind. The rock upon which she landed was sharp and cut the tight, swollen skin. Instantly the pressure from within the foot spurted out pus as well as the burr. In moments the swelling subsided and there was a noticeable improvement. Within two days the foot was nearly normal. Lady was completely armed again.

It was good to be back in the familiar valley. The friendly outline of the coastal mountains, the commanding view of Goat Mountain, and the lively waters of Peach Tree Creek were home. Out of habit, Lady glanced toward the coastal mountains, where the red-tile roof of her former residence was visible. Although it had been more than seven months since she had left, she still felt a tug inside whenever she looked at the house. There was a comfort about its presence

—a particle of her past that lingered on with pleasant memories.

The sound of pebbles falling drifted up from below and she knew even before she looked that it was the goat family. Things had changed little, but now to the east about three miles there was a strange difference in the land.

Later that day Lady drifted east to investigate the blackened hills. It was a strange landscape that floated beneath her. Stark skeletons of manzanita and madrone, black and gray ash several inches deep in places. Here and there skeletons and charred remains of victims. The vultures, condors, and ravens had done their job well; there was little left.

Scattered at random were pockets of grass or brush that, by some quirk of fate, had been untouched by the fire. These were little islands of vegetation in a sea of ash. In one of these islands she noticed a movement and swung around for another look. The brush rabbit moved again and exposed himself. This rabbit was one in a million, not just because he had survived the fire, but because he was almost completely white. Not a true albino but a mutation, which had left him with ninety percent of his fur snow white. Only a patch of rust color on his neck and part of his face were natural.

The rabbit was one from the previous spring and had survived only because he lived in such dense chaparral that he could find easy concealment. But now that his protective cover was gone, his time was limited.

Lady pitched down and began an attack run. The white rabbit saw the dark form of the eagle and reacted as any normal brush rabbit would. He crouched close to the ground beside a tuft of dry grass, his only cover. But it was a futile attempt to avoid detection since his white color stood out

123

like a banner against the brown grass. In seconds Lady had made the kill and mounted up to return with it to Goat Mountain. This was nature's way—natural selection—of ridding its species of unwanted traits. It had worked well. The white rabbit wasn't the only rabbit in the grass island. A normal-colored one crouched not more than twenty feet away as Lady began her run. The white color attracted her attention, however, and as a result, the rabbit possessing the undesirable mutant gene was eliminated.

For several days the two eagles renewed their acquaintance with familiar spots in the valley. Several times Lady returned to the lake to take a coot, until the flock changed their location to across the lake near a campground.

It was on one of these forays that Lady saw another eagle over the lake. Although it was on the fringe of her territory, she set off toward the intruder on a direct course. This flight was of special significance, since it was an identifying flight, a threat flight to let the intruding eagle know that he was trespassing.

For two miles she flew, not stopping to soar as usual. The other eagle was not of her species. It was the first bald eagle Lady had ever encountered. The immature male lacked the distinctive white head and tail of the familiar national emblem and to the casual eye he could easily have been mistaken for a golden eagle. But to Lady's eye he was of another species—nevertheless not welcome in her territory.

The bald eagle spotted her while she was yet a mile away and instantly recognized her threat flight. It wasn't his purpose to initiate a territorial dispute. At two years of age he was still wandering and wasn't interested in setting up a territory. In fact, he was the only bald eagle in this entire section of Southern California, although just fifteen years before, bald eagles had thrived along the coast and its off-shore islands. But owing to the pesticides absorbed into their bodies from eating contaminated fish, the reproduction rate for the species had been sharply cut. Now this lone male was one of the last of a dwindling species that is facing the same situation as the California condor.

Once the bald eagle recognized Lady's threat flight, he turned and headed across the lake, away from her territory. As soon as he had crossed the invisible boundary, Lady pulled up and began to soar. Just as her threat flight had been clearly understood by the bald eagle, so was her abrupt pull-up and soaring. He was no longer in her territory and was free to proceed unmolested. He continued across the lake and took a perch in a dead sycamore on the bluff.

The golden eagle feeds primarily on mammals but the bald eagle is a fisherman and has developed a fine technique for catching his water prey. As a result the natural habitat of the bald eagle is usually near large bodies of water. This particular male was raised along the Washington coast, where he learned to fish the rivers as they emptied into the sea. His wanderings had taken him southward along the coast, up rivers, and lake-hopping until he arrived at Cachuma Lake.

From his perch the eagle had an excellent view of the water surface. Unlike a pelican, who dives at great speed and is able to catch fish several feet beneath the surface, the bald eagle must catch his prey within a foot of the surface. Most of the species that make up his catch are the slower surface fish that fishermen seldom prize. The exception is in the northwest, during salmon season, when the eagles catch great quantities of the red-fleshed fish as they migrate up shallow rivers to spawn.

A school of sluggish goldfish swam lazily near the surface along the shore, three hundred yards to the west of the eagle. He watched them for several minutes before launching. His flight carried him out over the lake at two hundred feet altitude. The bald eagle has a particular problem that doesn't exist with most other predatory birds: Since his prey is beneath the water's surface, the sun's glare often makes it invisible. His approach, therefore, must be made from an angle that avoids the glare. Unlike the golden eagle, which can make low approaches, the bald eagle must maintain an elevation that will allow his eyes to penetrate the water.

Flying slowly, this young eagle approached the goldfish until he was nearly above them. Then he thinned his wings and dropped in a fast spiral, striking the water with extended talons. With his talons closed tightly around the fat body of a fish, he flapped his way from the surface. Once in the air, he headed for shore, changing his grip several times to streamline his burden. Finally, with the fish riding headfirst like an orange torpedo beneath its mother craft, he gained enough altitude to make the bluff.

From across the lake, Lady had watched the whole episode. She had never seen anything like it before. She recognized that the eagle had prey, for even now he was tearing into the white flesh. But she had never associated water with prey. To her, it was only a place to drink and bathe. She mounted up and headed for the back country. The bald eagle would remain here throughout the winter. The two eagles would frequently see each other, but they lived in two separate worlds.

The history of Lady's territory in California is richly steeped in Spanish and Mexican tradition, and even today the influence of these early people can be seen everywhere. Cities, towns, rivers, mountains, and valleys have names of Spanish origin. Architecture and even the way of life in the ranch country is reminiscent of the days when Mexican *vaqueros* rode the range. Gone are the vaqueros, the Mexican governors, and the grizzlies which once roamed the area. But then, as now, eagles hunted the valley.

Along the southern fringe of Lady's property ran the Santa Ynez River. At this late autumn date it was only a trickle, but a wide bed littered with well-worn rocks and drift debris indicated that at other times it wasn't so dry. In fact, the time wasn't far off when it would be raging with muddy, swirling waters.

An ancient oak that stood out prominently among younger trees along the bluff was another of Lady's favorite perching sites. Halfway between the lake and Goat Mountain, she often took advantage of the tree if the air was still and she wanted to rest before climbing up to get into the back country. This tree was probably the one nearest to habitation that she used, since across the riverbed, about half a mile, was one of the houses of the San Fernando Rey Ranch. The house was of no alarm to Lady, although her mate was shy of its proximity.

On this particular morning she had just finished feeding on a catch near the edge of the lake. Being too heavy to make it to Goat Mountain easily, she sat in the branches of this convenient tree.

Beneath the old oak, wedged between a fallen tree and the oak's broad trunk, was a huge pile of sticks nearly six feet high and almost ten feet wide. At first glance one might think it was purely a natural happening, a result of years of twigs and leaves falling or being blown into the spot. But closer examination revealed that the jumbled mass contained just a bit more order than chance could have provided. Small sticks and grasses were wedged in between the larger sticks to seal the structure. It was a wood rat's lodge and had been in more or less continuous use for nearly a hundred years. What original nest materials still existed now lay buried beneath layers of more recent vintage. On the very top were fresh twigs put there within the past few weeks. The entire structure had the appearance of just growing from the ground, the Western Hemisphere's equivalent to the giant anthills of Africa.

Within the lodge were several separate chambers with separate entrances. In spite of its huge size, the lodge housed only four rats, each in his own apartment, each completely independent of the others.

Living entirely in the woods, these rats are not to be confused with the Norway rat that infects city slums and garbage dumps, and spreads disease. The wood rat lives a relatively clean life, seldom coming into contact with man. He forages at night for acorns, seeds, and berries and hauls them to his lodge. A kleptomaniac, he will steal anything that suits his fancy, but often leaves a less desirable item in trade. Consequently his warehouse is often filled with treasures—smooth stones, pure white bones, pieces of tinfoil, and, at times, things of real value.

Not more than fifty yards away from the lodge was the location of an old camp where Chinese road workers on the San Marcos stage route had lived and practiced their traditional ways without harrassment from the other workers. During the time the Chinese lived there, many valuable items had mysteriously disappeared and many a finger was pointed in accusation. No one ever suspected Neotoma, the

128

trade rat, who slipped unobtrusively into camp each night and made off with some shiny object, leaving an acorn in return.

Over the years the shiny objects were traded by the rats from generation to generation, from lodge to lodge. Occasionally they exchanged a treasured item for "fool's gold"— a worthless object in the eyes of man but prized by the rat. Such was the case when an amateur treasure hunter arrived at the campsite nearly a hundred years after the Chinese left. After preliminary examination of the site, he left to return the next day. But before he left he accidentally dropped a foil gum wrapper.

Neotoma found the shiny wrapper in the moonlight and appropriated it, leaving a dull but valuable early American coin in its stead. Returning the next day with a metal detector, the treasure hunter soon found the coin. But search as he did, he could find no other. After spending the day with no further luck, he abandoned the site. Little did he know that a scant fifty yards away, within that jumbled pile of sticks, lay prizes that would delight the most serious treasure hunter. Before leaving he dropped another foil wrapper, but since he never returned, he never found out what new treasure Neotoma might have left.

It was midday before a breeze stirred around the ancient oak and Lady mounted up to return to the back country. It was getting overcast and a strange feeling was in the air.

chapter xii

Far out at sea, some three hundred miles to the northwest, a weather front was moving toward the Pacific coast. A low-pressure area had formed and with it a heavy altocumulus cloud cover. As the low-pressure area neared the coast, it gathered more moisture and soon a dark gray nimbus cloud layer formed closer to the surface. It was the first rainstorm of the season to strike the coast.

The wind, which all summer had flowed gently from the west, now began to change in a counterclockwise direction. Within a few hours it was blowing steadily from the southeast. As the atmospheric pressure dropped, the wind increased and a heavy cloud cover moved into the Santa Ynez Valley.

This change in weather conditions was noted by much of the wildlife. The smell of rain was in the air: a fresh, clean smell that brought with it the sense of change—a distinct change from autumn to winter.

The increase in wind and the sudden drop in temperature were invigorating to Lady. She mounted up to put the wind to use. There was an irresistible sudden urge to fly that was felt not only by Lady but by other birds as well. Ravens swooped back and forth across the leaden sky like black darts. Near the lake, several great blue herons soared gracefully along the shoreline. Forty miles to the south, along the coast, huge swarms of sea gulls left their usual low scavenging flight pattern to soar thousands of feet in the sky, calling nervously to each other. Even several Cooper's hawks and a sharp-shinned hawk, the agile, swift predators of the woodlands, soared high above the valley. For several hours this extraordinary assortment of flying creatures moved with uncertainty about the sky.

The first few drops of rain seemed to wake these creatures from their hypnotic state and one by one they returned to their normal habitat to resume their role in nature. The rain began softly at first, each drop sending up a small cloud of dust as it hit the dry earth. Soon the dustiness of summer was hidden beneath a dark cloak of moisture.

Bit by bit the drops passed between thick clusters of oak leaves, catching on each leaf momentarily, then running to another, washing each in turn. Finally large, dirty drops broke loose from the lowermost leaves to land loudly amidst dead leaves beneath the tree. Down by the ancient oak, a few drops on the roof of the wood rats' lodge caused a stir within. Already restless because of the atmospheric pressure change, one of the rats emerged, with quivering nose, to investigate. He was only visible for a moment, but it was long enough for the Cooper's hawk, sheltering in the oak, to dart down and snatch up the unfortunate rodent.

By now a soft, gray mist covered the valley. Lady pitched down and headed for a convenient perch, the rain pelting her body, but at the last minute she changed course and headed for the creek, where she landed on a rain-washed rock. For some unexplained reason this kind of weather always brought on the urge to bathe. During her years in captivity, she had always responded to stormy weather by bathing, much to the bewilderment of her trainer. Now she hopped into the water and in moments was soaking wet. Shaking herself, she climbed with difficulty up out of the canyon and took a perch on the protected northwest side of a cliff. For the rest of the day she huddled against the cliff, trying, with little luck, to dry off.

For two days the rain fell steadily, at times driven with great force by the wind. Groups of deer lay in clusters beneath dense oaks to escape the rain. Small birds, such as finches and juncos, perched in the thick brush for protection. Everywhere, wildlife waited patiently for a letup.

The water of Peach Tree Creek was muddy as it dashed toward the river. The Santa Ynez River itself already showed evidence of the storm. No longer a clear trickle, it now was a respectable river.

On the third day it cleared briefly and the wet rocks steamed as the sun's rays warmed them. The towhees, juncos, and other ground-feeding birds flocked to the level areas where water runoff had deposited seeds and insects carried down from the slopes.

But the respite from the rain was only a few hours; barely enough time for Lady to take a jackrabbit that had been flushed from dense brush by a coyote. Another storm was following closely on the heels of the first. The gentle rain of the first storm had been welcomed by the people of the area. It had been just enough to germinate the seeds which had been sowed by helicopter over the burned area. Now, the Forest Service was concerned that severe erosion and flooding would occur as a result of the fire's destruction of watershed.

The gathering clouds and darkening sky were ominous—low enough that the tip of Goat Mountain was completely obscured. All around the valley's perimeter clouds played tag with the hilltops. Other clouds hung silent and brooding as if pondering their enormous task of watering the earth. The winds increased in velocity, carrying with them a mixture of leaves, dry grasses, and other mementos of summer.

Just below the gray ceiling, five hundred feet above the valley floor, Lady soared on half-closed wings, bouncing back and forth in the rough air, in a flight that was far from the lazy soaring on gentle summer breezes. Here was challenge, a matching of wits against the elements in which she used all the facilities nature had provided her. A mere third of her flight surfaces were in use. An abrupt bump that pushed her to the left was countered by pulling in the right wing and extending the left. An instant later it was just the opposite. She was constantly shifting, countering, changing altitudes and configurations. A sudden surge up and, just as sudden, a drop as the air rose and fell like a tumultuous sea. She thrilled in the experience! A sudden upcurrent swept her aloft at incredible speed, carrying her instantly into a world of white nothingness. For a moment she was startled at the sudden loss of orientation. For several seconds she fought the currents, striving to maintain her position. It was un-

familiar and frightening, being in a cloud. Folding her wings, she plummeted straight down through the blinding mist. In seconds she burst from the cloud, dropping like a missile, back to the world of earth and sky.

Suddenly a thunderous roar struck the valley, causing the very air itself to vibrate. The thunder echoed back and forth across the canyon for half a minute. Moments later, frozen droplets of rain began to pelt the earth. The hailstones fell with increasing velocity from the leaden sky. Still several hundred feet above the valley, Lady was suddenly pounded by hundreds of pellets. Never before had she experienced a hailstorm while in flight. The deluge of pea-sized crystals pounded her literally to the ground. She was forced to seek a place of shelter before she suffered injury. Moments later she huddled close against a cliff, while the white pebbles bounced and danced across the land.

Within minutes the hail covered the ground, in some places several inches deep. Just as suddenly as it had begun, the hail stopped and huge drops of rain began to fall. The rest of that day it poured. All night and on into the next day the rain continued. Peach Tree Creek was already up to its banks and many heretofore dry creek beds were now running wild. Down the hillsides the water cascaded, forming hundreds of tiny waterfalls as it dashed for the river.

To the east, where the fire had stripped the hills, the water rushed down slopes with absolutely no resistance. Rivulets and streamlets, black with ashes, gouged into the unprotected earth. Valuable topsoil, which had taken thousands of years to form, was washed into the valleys below.

Debris, consisting of tons of dry twigs and loose rocks, was swept down gullies to be snagged at various places. More debris, in turn, was collected and soon these natural dams caused water to back up, forming temporary ponds. As the level rose in one of the ponds, crevices and holes never before subjected to water were inundated.

Beneath a ledge, a narrow, low slit in the hill provided a hibernating den for Pacific rattlesnakes. Even now, as the water rose, two dozen of the dormant reptiles lay intertwined in a living mass of cold plastic flesh. The water crept slowly into the den, encircled the snakes, and eventually engulfed them. But in their state of dormancy they hardly noticed it, and even though submerged, many would survive.

An hour later the pressure on the dam was too great and the mass of debris broke loose with a loud roar, sending a raging torrent of churning water down into the canyon. The level in the pond dropped rapidly. As the snake den drained, the mass of reptiles was carried out and down the creek.

The snakes weren't the only creatures rudely awakened from their winter sleep. As the water flowed across flatlands, it poked into every hole and burrow. Tarantula spiders, secure in their shallow holes, were the first to go. Water swirled down squirrel holes like water down a bath drain. Some squirrels were trapped; others managed by sheer luck to find a free opening. One squirrel struggled heroically against the current as he tried to exit his hole. But, with the entrance in sight, he collapsed and was carried back into the depths of the burrow.

Not far away a smaller burrow housed a pocket gopher who slept snugly beneath closed doors. A nocturnal underground dweller, the gopher always plugged his hole entrance for the daylight hours. This habit had so far saved him from the rushing water above. But the earthen door could only withstand the prying of the water for thirty minutes. Then, with a triumphant gurgle, the water made its

137

sinister way below. The gopher instantly sensed the intrusion and dashed for the open door, intending to plug it. A third of the way up he met the onrushing water. Digging deep into the earthen walls with his sharp claws, the plucky rodent fought his way ahead. At the very edge of the entrance, the water threatened to dislodge him but he gripped harder, even stabbing his large front teeth into the ground. With herculean effort he pulled himself free of the current and scurried out on the surface, angry at the unseen enemy that had routed him. After much grinding of his big yellow teeth and other threatening display, he went his soggy way, searching for a new home.

On the oak-covered slopes near the creek several wild pigs rooted in the leaf mulch, oblivious to the downpour. The sudden deluge had brought to the surface scores of insects, larvae, and other subterranean dwellers and the pigs were feasting on them joyously. One member of the group had wandered across a dry wash and was busy feeding when, with a roar, water gushed down the wash as a debris dam broke above. The sudden noise frightened the near-grown pig and he charged across the wash toward the others and the safety of the trees. Without hesitating, he plunged into the water and was instantly swept away, squealing loudly and trying desperately to paddle with his short legs. In moments he had disappeared over a waterfall and was lost in the raging torrent while the other pigs, engrossed in their work, did not even lift a head at their comrade's plight.

In a large oak at the edge of a clearing a great horned owl huddled close against the damp trunk, trying futilely to sleep. The constant buffeting of the wind and the splattering of huge raindrops against his feathers kept the nocturnal predator awake. With half-opened eyes the owl stared down into the field below. The appearance of the pocket gopher wandering erratically about, looking for a hole, caught his attention. Although it was daylight, and he was not wont to hunt by day, the owl's interest was captured. He hadn't eaten well the last two days and the easy prey below was tempting. On silent wings he swooped out of the oak and in a single movement snatched the wandering rodent in a vise-like grip and returned to the tree.

Down by the wood rats' lodge the runoff followed the easiest course to flow into the Santa Ynez River. Each small gully or deer trail became a temporary guide for the water. The rat lodge was in an excellent location, being on a rise with a swale ten yards to the east. In years past, heavy runoff water had always flowed down the swale, leaving the lodge dry. But only the year before an old, decayed oak had fallen and one huge limb lay across the swale. Now debris was collecting against it and water was backing up. Soon the water would have to seek another way to the river.

Within the lodge, the four tenants slept soundly and dry, completely secure against the elements. Their security, how-ever, would last only as long as the water flowed away from the lodge. And now, as it backed up behind the fallen tree, the water began to follow the path of least resistance. Count-less years of rats going to and from the lodge had left several well-worn trails, one of which the water now followed. In minutes it had flowed into the lodge, routing the tenants. Now each stood atop his apartment, looking around in be-wilderment. Little by little the water surrounded the lodge and pried gently but firmly at its foundations.

Not all the creatures of the valley were adversely affected by the rain. Ravens, their black bodies glistening in the dull light, bounced across the ground at the base of gullies. They jabbed with their sharp beaks at large crickets, beetles, and even lizards, whose privacy had been sluiced away.

In the willow thickets along the creek, several raccoons caught salamanders that had been routed from beneath rocks and logs by the rising water. The swirling water had brought with it all sorts of good things that would delight even the most discriminating raccoon.

In the meager shelter of the cliff, Lady and Patu spent the entire day. They had some protection from the wind but the cliff did little to keep the rain off. With feathers fluffed, the two birds stood side by side, staring off into the valley. Hour after hour they stood, shifting periodically from one leg to the other. Their sharp eyes watched the ground below but, even though they saw prey, they had little interest. They would wait out the storm.

As darkness fell, the air got colder and the rain slackened a bit. The runoff, however, continued to inundate portions of the valley. For several hours it had pried at the wood rats' lodge. One of the rats had vacated the besieged lodge and was perched safely above in the oak. The lodge was now almost completely undermined. The three remaining rats had dug into the roof top and were fairly well situated. But little by little the earth surrounding the lodge began to crumble, and stick by stick the foundations of the structure were washed away. Around midnight the entire lodge lurched as it dropped into the eroded excavation. No longer supported by the oak's trunk, it began to disintegrate.

The three rats had waited too long and were trapped in the lodge. Foot by foot, the lodge moved toward the bluff, dissolving decades of work as it progressed. By two-thirty in the morning only a remnant of the structure was left. Only one rat remained; the others had fled off into the current and been swept away. Now the last tenant clung precariously to his dissolving home, determined to hang on to this last vestige of safety. Then, without warning, the last bit disappeared over the bluff. Just before dawn the rain ceased and with it the wind.

chapter xiii

For the first time in five days, the sun's full rays fell on the soaked valley. Although the air was cold and the clouds hung threateningly around the mountain peaks, it was a welcome relief from the previous week.

As soon as the first rays hit the earth, Patu and Lady flew to an exposed spot and began to preen and dry. For over an hour they stood with wings drooped and backs to the sun. In the cold air, steam rose from their damp feathers and curled upward above their heads.

The valley around them showed the results of over nine inches of rain in five days. This was an area which measured no more than fifteen or twenty inches of rain the entire year. The loss of the watershed to the east had accentuated the runoff. At the base of each canyon was a fan-shaped accumulation of mud and rock similar to the alluvial fans often seen at the mouth of desert mountain canyons. The stream bed of Peach Tree Creek had been altered and was even now changing course by the hour.

The fast of over three days had left Lady with an aggressive appetite. She launched into the wind and climbed rapidly to a thousand feet. She was alert and sharp. She felt light and capable. Several times she stooped and pulled up sharply in a flight pattern reminiscent of courtship. She was conscious of Patu watching and, although it was only December, they were both beginning to feel the first gentle whispering of spring.

The cold air was thick and responded quickly to her flight surfaces. She swung in a high arc to the southeast, over Loma Alta Peak and across Redrock Canyon, which drains runoff from Old Man Mountain. She was interested in the burned-over area, remembering the easy catch of the albino brush rabbit. The black slopes looked sloppy and strange. In places whole sides of the hill had been eroded away, leaving raw wounds on the surface. The area looked lifeless and she turned southwest, keeping her altitude. Behind her and a bit lower she saw her mate spiraling upward. She circled until he joined her; then the two eagles worked southward.

Out of habit they followed the Santa Ynez River to the west, using the air currents that were deflected upward along the steep canyon at this point. Once the river left the canyon, it spread out and only then did the two eagles notice the change.

The river was swollen to its full width of over a hundred yards, with muddy, churning water. An incredible mass of logs and heavy brush was being carried along with the current. Here and there an entire tree rode the current in an upright position as its heavy rootball balanced it perfectly. Some small birds perched in the tree, as casually as if it were still firmly rooted to the ground. The debris of humans was also caught in the swirling mass. Barrels, old refrigerators, and miscellaneous junk were bobbing their way along, the results of man's illegal dumping of refuse upstream.

Two miles downriver, the entire mass slowed as the water entered the upper portion of Cachuma Lake. Here was as chaotic and awesome a situation as one could imagine, stark evidence of the power of nature. Thousands of tons of debris were jammed so hard against each other that one could practically walk on it. Giant logs of timber obviously had made a journey of many miles from the higher elevations where such timber existed. Countless stumps and dead chaparral that had lain in dry washes for decades floated in the muck.

Scattered throughout the flotsam were the victims. The bloated body of the pig floated in the tangled root of a tree. Several deer carcasses and a lifeless steer bobbed nearby. And, almost unbelievably, amid the mass a movement of life appeared. A wood rat had ridden out the entire trip, clinging to a log. Several times he had been submerged, but in absolute terror he had clung to the wood. Now he rose up to look quizzically about him at the quiet, undulating surface.

A small oak tree floated fifty yards to the north of the rat. It was the only familiar thing the rat could see and he set out on a precarious journey to gain the safety of the tree—from one log raft to another, and across an old root burl. It was wet and slippery but he forged on, eyes fixed on the bobbing oak. He paused momentarily on a cottonwood stump and didn't notice that not more than two feet away was the shiny body of a Pacific rattlesnake entwined about the root. Amazingly, the reptile was still alive and moving,

144

but too cold and inactive to be a threat. With another bound the rat made it to a floating power pole, and then on to the oak. There he would stay until the tree beached itself. Well provisioned with a good supply of green leaves, he would survive his ordeal.

From her high altitude Lady had a good view of the strange scene below. Her attention was diverted, however, to the black forms of coots that had clambered aboard some of the flotsam instead of forging out on their usual bank. It was a simple trick to snare one before he made it into the water. Both Lady and Patu were successful.

For the next several weeks the weather remained clear and cold. Winter is brief in this area and hardly has it begun when it is over. Only once, during January, did the country-side resemble winter as wildlife in other parts of the country know it.

A local front moved in about midday, with cold temperatures hovering around freezing. There was not the fanfare there had been with the big storm in December—only quiet, brooding clouds close to the ground. During the night the proper conditions were met and a light snowfall began.

On her cliffside perch, Lady slept soundly through the night, awakening just before dawn. For over an hour she stood unmoving in the gathering light, anticipating the new day. But the ground looked strangely different. In all her seventeen years, this was only the second time she had ever experienced snow. Her reaction was much the same as it had been on that first occasion, where she was only three, at the Grand Canyon in Arizona. Now, as then, she was intrigued with the white stuff.

She looked about her, leaned over, and bit at a clump of

snow that had formed on a rock below her. She tasted its cold wetness and shook her bill. Slowly her feathers rose and she roused vigorously, sending flurries of snow swirling in all directions. As she launched from the cliff, millions of glittering crystals were sent tumbling. Mounting up again atop the cliff, she hopped off onto the rock and shuffled through the two-inch-deep snow.

Frequently she bent down to bite the crystalline cold, then flicked her bill clear. Like a young colt, she bounced and pranced through the snow, excited by the new element. At times she lashed out savagely to crush a snowball in her talons, or chased a snow chunk that tried to escape her. It was invigorating fun and she was thoroughly pleased with herself. By afternoon much of the white stuff had mysteriously disappeared; she would have to wait another year to experience it again.

Even with the melting of the snow one could discern a change in the ground, as small green bits of vegetation began to appear. The days were lengthening ever so little and the wildlife began to respond. On the blackened slopes to the east a remarkable change was taking place. In addition to the helicopter-scattered seeds, many varieties of chaparral were already germinating. Certain species of chaparral have seeds that lie dormant for years and can only germinate after being exposed to intense heat. Other species have large root crowns at ground level that survive fire and sprout new stems after the first rain. It is nature's way of ensuring rapid regrowth after a fire. Now the hillsides began to take on a tinge of green; life was returning.

The longer daylight and the warmer temperatures triggered many a biological clock in the myriads of creatures in the valley. In Peach Tree Creek, the eggs of the dragonfly had hatched. The nymphs began their predacious life of several weeks beneath the surface before emerging to undergo the miracle of metamorphosis.

The cycles of every creature were perfectly synchronized. The dragonflies wouldn't emerge until there were newly hatched insects for them to prey on. Thousands of insect-feeding warblers and kinglets that had spent the winter in Central America would arrive in the valley coincidentally with the insect crop. The appearance of the new grasses could always be expected to coincide with the birth of young rodents, who need the tender shoots. And concurrently, the arrival of the young rodents coincides with the predators' annual nesting.

Even now, in mid-February, a large female great horned owl sat on a nest in a huge sycamore in Horse Canyon. The year before the nest had been used by ravens, but the early-nesting owl would have her family nearly raised before the ravens were ready. In a few days her youngsters would hatch and she would begin preying upon the new crop of rodents.

Down at the lake, the flock of Canada geese was getting restless. One day, at the end of February, they left for their nesting grounds in Oregon. Great blue herons were congregating around a tall stand of sycamore trees on the east bank. Soon their large, bulky nests would dot the treetops and a heron apartment would be started. Of course, the heron youngsters would arrive just in time for their parents to take advantage of the new generation of fish and frogs.

On the unburned hillsides, huge thickets of Ceanothus—wild lilac—was already in purple bloom, a source of food for newly hatched butterflies and honeybees. There was no wasted energy as every plant and animal species began the annual drive to regenerate its own kind.

The biological timepiece within Lady and Patu had also rung its alarm. Every day now was filled with breathtaking plunges from dizzy heights as the pair of eagles engaged in the age-old ritual of courtship. Their loud calls echoed across the canyons, causing a soft-eyed doe with swollen sides to look up at the sound. It was this call, with its mellow, haunting quality, that held the secret of survival of the species. Without it, there could be no procreation of golden eagles.

With outstretched wings, Lady hung motionless two thousand feet above the valley, her large wings easily supporting her in the gentle updraft. The large primary features curved gracefully upward at the tips as the air flowed past. From slightly above and behind, Patu approached and passed within two feet of her. She uttered a low, twittering call and he answered. Her very presence excited him and he responded by giving the mating call. Then he dropped a thousand feet before shooting up again like a moon-bound missile. Minutes later he drifted away to skirt a distant cliff. Lady made no move to follow. It was his duty to locate a nest site. Once he had two or three picked out, she would be happy to check them over. She swung to the west, toward Santa Cruz Canyon.

At the edge of the lake, in a small protected bay, a pied-billed grebe was answering the call. Bit by bit she hauled pieces of grass, reeds, and small twigs into the center of the bay. There, in a marvel of engineering, she anchored the material to a reed and constructed her floating nest. Each piece added to the buoyancy of the raft. After two days of diligent work, the grebe climbed aboard the wobbly platform. A day later she laid six white eggs and set down to a period of incubation.

Lady pitched down steeply toward the edge of the lake and swooped in low over a stand of rushes. As she cleared the reeds, the startled grebe dived headlong off its nest into the water. But the grebe was not the eagle's objective; a drake mallard, preoccupied with the courting of a dusky female, was her target. The drake scarcely knew what hit him as Lady dropped abruptly from over the reeds.

With the return of spring the fields were again active with ground squirrels. At many holes, small pairs of eyes peered inquisitively out at the bright world for the first time. In a few days the young squirrels would be allowed to emerge topside and take their chances along with the others.

Up an oak-covered canyon, beneath a huge tangle of rotten logs and poison oak, the old sow nursed her dozen naked piglets. They would stay in the thicket for a week or more before venturing forth with their mother to face the hazards of life.

Several miles to the east, along a rimrock on Old Man Mountain, the cougar also nursed her youngsters. Three kittens had been born but one died the first day. The remaining two were healthy, fat, furry balls, already expressing playfulness. The mother cat lay on her side, purring, while the kittens satisfied themselves. Then, while they played with her tail, she dozed.

For the third time, Patu offered a nest site to Lady. Their site of the previous year wasn't acceptable, since during the December storm a portion of the cliff had been dislodged and the ledge no longer existed. The second site he selected was an old red-tailed hawks' nest and was a bit too crowded for Lady's needs. The third site was on a steep cliff that had been formed years before, when earth tremors had caused severe slippage. This location pleased Lady and she accepted, much to Patu's delight.

It was toward evening when she arrived at the nest site with a fistful of twigs. Then Patu arrived with a bushy twig in his bill and, with great pride, placed it on the ledge. For ten minutes Lady arranged and rearranged the few sticks. In the gathering gloom, the two birds paused to survey their work. From down in the canyon the evening call of the California quail could be heard. On the darkened slopes below, hundreds of yucca lifted their white-blossomed heads like lighted candles. In the evening twilight the eagles on the ledge were barely visible. It apparently satisfied them well for they elected to roost there that night.

The sun-warmed earth responded eagerly to spring as countless shrubs burst into bloom and grasses grew almost visibly. Hordes of birds arrived daily in the valley, some to remain, others to follow spring further north.

Down by the creek, hundreds of cliff swallows had just completed their long journey up the Pacific coast from South America. Now, amid a noisy din of creaking notes, they gathered mud from the stream bank to construct their jug-like dwellings on the cliff above. In an amazingly short time the cliff became a mass of wall-to-wall adobe dwellings.

A beautiful hermit warbler, with bright yellow head, landed briefly on a rock amid the swallows, drank deeply, and hurried on. Although he had already flown twenty-four hundred miles from Nicaragua, he still had nine hundred miles to go to a woodland stream edge in Washington.

The early fruits of the bayberry bushes that grew in profusion along the edge of a clearing drew the attention of swarms of cedar waxwings. The handsome, well-groomed birds consumed every berry on the bushes within a few hours, before moving up the mountain and finally on into the northern portion of the state where they would nest.

A male bobcat, prowling along a brushy ridge, was startled one morning as a dark shadow passed overhead. He crouched silently as Lady spiraled down toward the bush. Although he was ready to defend himself, it wasn't necessary. Lady was only on a nest-building mission. Flapping hard, she hovered just above the dry shrub and ripped off a fistful of twigs. In an instant she was gone.

Day by day the pile of twigs took shape. As work progressed on the nest, the size and types of materials changed —from inch-thick sticks at first, to soft grasses near the completion. Countless times Lady returned with soft grasses pulled from the fields below. The time had almost arrived; the cradle was ready. Several times she and Patu had copulated and now the shells were forming around the viable embryos. On March 15 she ovulated and shortly thereafter began the long, inactive period of incubation.

epilogue

Against the irregular pattern of the mud cliff the nest was nearly invisible. The brooding eagle who set low in the nest could not be seen from below, and her mate stayed prudently away lest the site be revealed.

For Lady, this nesting season was of special significance. Although she wasn't aware of it, she had almost completed an entire year away from captivity. It had been a year in which she had learned how to cope with a wild life—learning her capabilities as well as her limitations. Although she had had a brief and almost disastrous encounter with man's influence in the environment, she had experienced to the fullest the joy of freedom to wander as the spirit moved her. Now the sights and sounds of the four seasons had become part of her life.

For sixteen years the instinctive fear of man had lain secreted within her genes—unrecognized. During the last year this latent fear had gradually surfaced. Generations of eagles before her had experienced persecution by man, and now the results of their experience had, by some mysterious miracle, been handed down to Lady.

As long as she lives, Lady will be a part of this valley. Although she is seventeen years old, she may well live another twenty. Her only threat is man and his insatiable appetite for land and its resources. Over the years the golden eagle has been flushed from its ancestral hunting and nesting grounds and forced to seek less desirable areas. Even now, covetous eyes look toward the eagles' remaining strongholds.

For as long as man has been on earth the eagle has been a source of admiration. The ancient wise man Solomon declared that the way of an eagle was too wonderful for him to understand. Modern man, by contrast, is often too busy to turn his eyes skyward. In his apathy, he goes his way, not realizing his loss.

It has been nearly forty days since incubation began. Lady is stiff and sluggish from inactivity. Suddenly, her eyes spot a movement far off in the sky. A foreign sound intrudes on the solitude. The eagle watches as the small aircraft approaches and skirts the cliff. She doesn't recognize it as being part of man, only a noisy intrusion. The airplane draws closer and in a moment passes over her cliff. She crouches low and looks up as it passes. There is a subconscious familiarity about the sight and sound.

The pilot scans the cliff and spots the nesting eagle. He swings around for another look. This flight is the first of the annual pilgrimages that he will make back into the valley. For sixteen years he and the nesting eagle below were close friends. And as with human friends who keep in touch by cards at Christmas, he will keep in touch with Lady once each year. She, of course, is unaware of the connection. For her it is long past. The two of them now live in different worlds.

As the plane recedes into the distance Lady feels a stir beneath her. Rising up slightly, she studies the mottled egg. A tiny hole has appeared and a faint peep comes from within. She responds in motherly fashion. A new life is beginning. She has fulfilled her supreme role in nature, that of propagating her species. She has reclaimed her rightful heritage. What lies ahead for Lady and her eaglets in a hostile world, only God knows.